# TECHNICAL
# WRITING
## FOR
## BUSINESS
## AND
## INDUSTRY

# TECHNICAL
# WRITING
## FOR
## BUSINESS
## AND
## INDUSTRY

Pamela S. Beason
Patricia A. Williams

SCOTT, FORESMAN AND COMPANY
Glenview, Illinois    London

Beason, Pamela S.
    Technical writing for business and industry / Pamela S. Beason,
Patricia A. Williams.
        p.    cm.
    Includes index.
    ISBN 0-673-38730-5
    1. Business writing.   2. Technical writing.   3. English language—
Business English.   4. English language—Technical English.
I. Williams, Patricia A.        II. Title.
HF5718.3.B42   1990
808′.066651——dc20                                        89-10296
                                                          CIP


    1 2 3 4 5 6 MPC  94 93 92 91 90 89

    ISBN 0-673-38730-5

Scott, Foresman professional books are available for bulk sales at quantity discounts.
For information, please contact Marketing Manager, Professional Books Group,
Scott, Foresman and Company, 1900 East Lake Avenue, Glenview, IL 60025.

To my mother, who taught me how to get things done.

P.B.

To Mike.

P.W.

# CONTENTS

PART TWO

## OUTLINING YOUR DOCUMENT    95

# 5

Classification and Partition                                                98
Subordination                                                              99
Logical Order                                                              100
   Chronological Order  100  /  Spatial Order  100  /
   Order of Importance  101  /  Order of
   Utility  101  /  General-to-Specific Order  102  /
   Specific-to-General Order  102  /  Simple-to-
   Complex Order  102  /  Cause-to-Effect
   Order  103  /  Effect-to-Cause Order  103  /
   Problem-Causes-Solution Order  104  /
   Compare-and-Contrast Order  104  /  Familiar-
   to-Unfamiliar Order  105  /  Acceptable-to-
   Unacceptable Order  105

# 6

# 7

# 10

# 11

# 15

## The Final Draft   253

# 16

## Sample Documents   261

# INTRODUCTION

As the demand for technical documents grows, the demand for writers grows, and more and more people from diverse backgrounds find themselves producing technical documents. Engineers are writing alternatives analyses, biologists are writing research reports, computer specialists are writing feasibility studies, chemists are writing grant proposals, and, every work day, supervisors, technicians, operators, and managers are writing all kinds of progress reports, proposals, recommendations, and justifications.

*Technical Writing for Business and Industry: A Practical Guide* presents the basics of technical writing for both experienced writers and novices. If you're an experienced technical writer, this book will show you some new approaches as well as remind you of the tried-and-true ones. If you're just beginning to write technical documents, this book will show you how, step by step.

Whatever your background, if you write technical documents, *Technical Writing for Business and Industry* can help. It has concrete, practical information to make writing easier and documents better. Step-by-step guidelines will help you plan and write technical documents with confidence.

*Technical Writing for Business and Industry* shows how to plan and write:

Research reports

Feasibility studies

Alternatives analyses

Recommendations

Memos

Instructional materials

Proposals

Promotional Materials

The book features a modular approach to planning and writing. Each type of document is made up of sets of modules. Decide which modules are appropriate for your document, write them one by one, assemble them, and you have created a comprehensive and effective document. The modular approach takes the guesswork out of the writing process.

You will also find helpful checklists throughout the book that you can use to prod your memory before you begin each phase of planning, organizing, and writing.

We designed this book to help you get the job done. We have taken the most useful theories and reduced them to their practical applications. We've organized the information in the order you'll need it as you go through the process of writing a document. You can read the book straight through to gain an in-depth understanding of the whole process, or you can turn to one of the parts listed below for specific information.

| | |
|---|---|
| *Part I*<br>*Planning Your*<br>*Document* | Gives an overview of the common types of technical documents and the modules they contain; describes the process of creating a document; tells how to make a document plan, create a schedule, decide on illustrations and layout, and create a style guide. |
| *Part II*<br>*Outlining Your*<br>*Document* | Shows how to outline the most common types of technical documents; includes at least one example of an outline for each type. |
| *Part III*<br>*Writing Your Document* | Tells how to compose paragraphs; link ideas with transitions; write from the readers' point of view; choose clear and strong language; write definitions, descriptions, explanations, instructions, and persuasive arguments. |
| *Part IV*<br>*Reviews and Revisions* | Shows how to use reviews to improve documents; describes the process of revising drafts and tells how to prepare the final draft for reproduction or printing. |

*Sample Documents*        Provides two examples—
                          a memo and a feasibility
                          study—with the modules fully
                          developed and in place.
                          Includes examples of tables of
                          contents, abstracts, indexes, and
                          the other modules in the front
                          and back matter.

*Technical Writing for Business and Industry* can't take all of the work out of technical writing, but it can make writing effective documents much easier.

# PART ONE

# PLANNING YOUR DOCUMENT

# Technical Documents and Their Modules

In today's workplace, technical writers are called on to write a variety of documents. We describe the most common types and show you how they're made up of interconnected modules. Once you know how to organize and write these documents, listed below, you'll be prepared to handle any and all technical writing assignments.

- ○ Reports
   Studies and Research Reports
   Feasibility Studies
   Alternatives Analyses
   Recommendations

- ○ Instructional Materials

- ○ Proposals

- ○ Memos

- ○ Promotional Materials

At first, the outline for a document may seem complex and involved. But by using the modular approach, you can break down a document into manageable segments for easier planning, organizing, and writing.

## THE MODULAR APPROACH

Anyone who struggles through the creation of their first few technical documents soon discovers that documents are the sum of their parts. You write a comprehensive explanation, for example, and then realize you need an introduction. Or you get the procedures in a user's guide down pat, then find you have to backtrack to list the equipment your readers will need. Each type of document has a recognizable pattern made up of parts, or modules, that fit together to make a satisfactory whole.

Almost all technical documents have two major modules, front matter and main text, which, in turn, are made up of smaller modules. Figure 1.1 shows the standard mod-

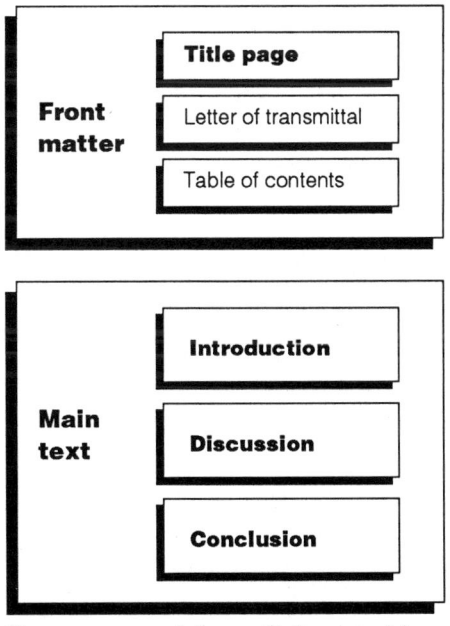

**Necessary modules** Optional modules

**Figure 1.1.** Standard Modules in Simple Documents.

ules found in nearly every document. Larger or more complex documents contain these standard modules plus some optional ones and may also contain back matter, a third large module. These are shown in Figure 1.2.

The way you organize and write modules for front matter stays pretty much the same from document to document. You can see examples of front matter modules—title page, letter of transmittal, approvals, distribution list, preface, table of contents, list of figures (and tables), and an abstract—in the sample document given in Chapter 16. The sample document also includes examples for back matter: an appendix, references, and an index.

Organizing and writing the main text, however, is what we concentrate on in this book. To create the main text, you write modules for an introduction, a discussion, and a conclusion. To create one of these modules, you write several smaller modules.

For example, look at the smaller modules in the discussion part of a research report shown in Figure 1.3.

You divide your discussion into as many topic modules as you need. You cover each topic by first defining it and then presenting your supporting information. You may then either summarize each topic after you present it or summarize all of them at the end of the discussion.

The modules you'd use for the discussion part of a research report are not the same ones you'd use in a feasibility study, a user's guide, or an alternatives analysis. Each type of document requires a different set of modules.

The following sections describe and diagram the five document types. You'll see what modules to include and how to arrange them. In Part Two, "Outlining Your Document," numerous examples show you how to organize specific documents. Part Three, "Writing Your Document," has guidelines to help you write your own modules and numerous examples that show you how to apply the guidelines.

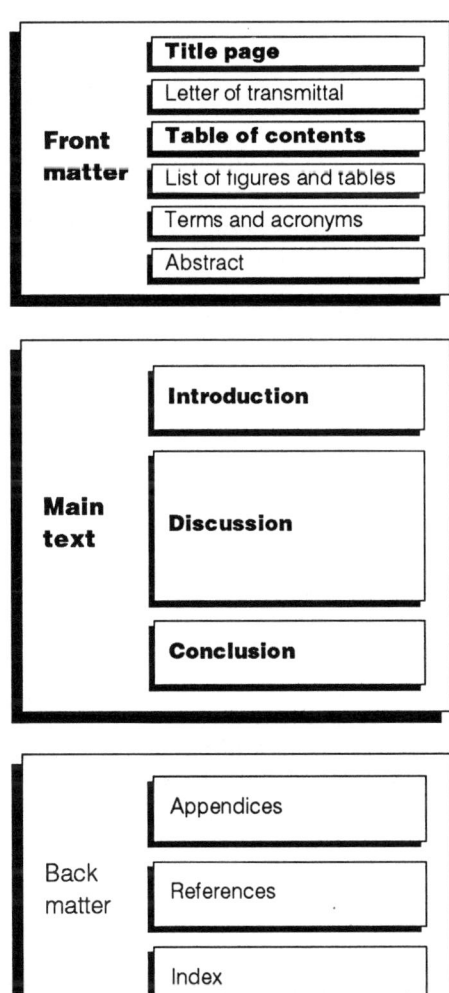

**Front matter**
- Title page
- Letter of transmittal
- Table of contents
- List of figures and tables
- Terms and acronyms
- Abstract

**Main text**
- Introduction
- Discussion
- Conclusion

**Back matter**
- Appendices
- References
- Index

**Necessary modules**    Optional modules

**Figure 1.2.**  Standard and Optional Modules in Longer or Complex Documents.

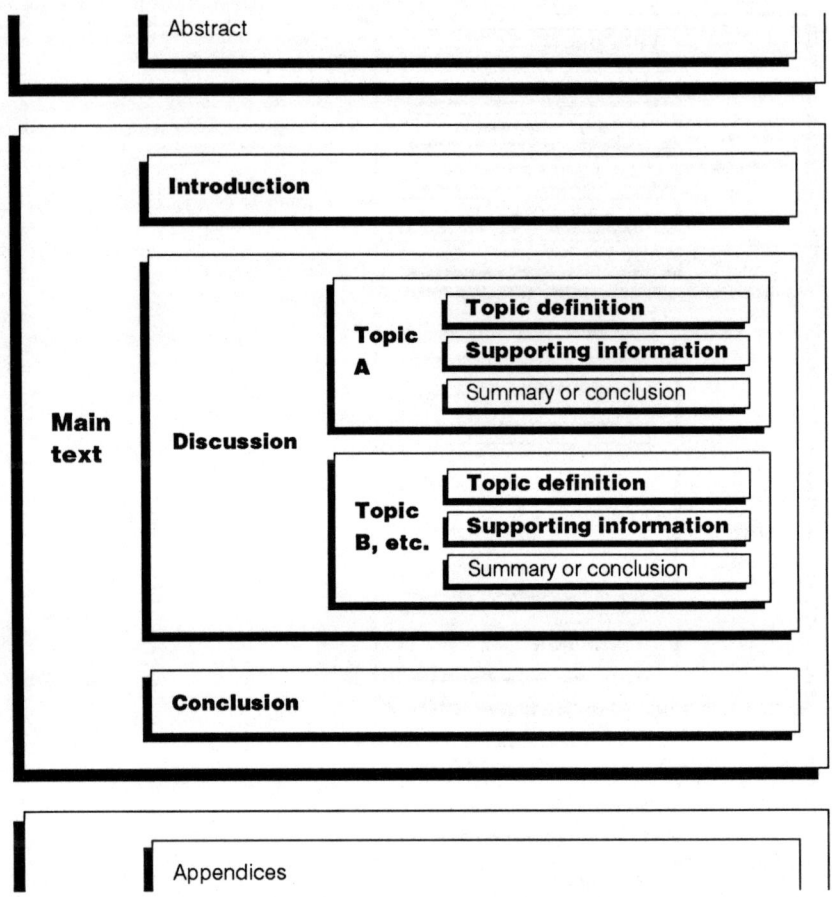

**Figure 1.3.** Details in a Research Report.

## REPORTS

Of the many types of reports, we cover the most common ones: studies and research reports, alternatives analyses, recommendations, and feasibility studies. You'll find sample outlines and diagrams of the modules for these types of reports in Chapter 6, "Outlining Reports and Memos."

Figure 1.4 diagrams a typical report, showing how it is organized by modules.

### STUDIES AND RESEARCH REPORTS

Studies and research reports, as their names imply, present the results of research and studies. They inform, explain, describe, and analyze. Sometimes they include conclusions and recommendations. They have titles like "The Effect of Proposition 33 on Production Costs," "How Circles Improved Profits," or "The Mating Habits of the Two-Toed Sloth."

### ALTERNATIVES ANALYSES

Alternatives analyses describe how a method or a product compares to other methods or products according to specific criteria. They have titles like "An Analysis of CAD/CAM Systems for Design and Development" or "The Direct vs. the Indirect Method."

### FEASIBILITY STUDIES

Feasibility studies analyze a proposed method, service, or product according to need, impact, risk, and cost. A study title might be "The Feasibility of Installing Central Word Processing."

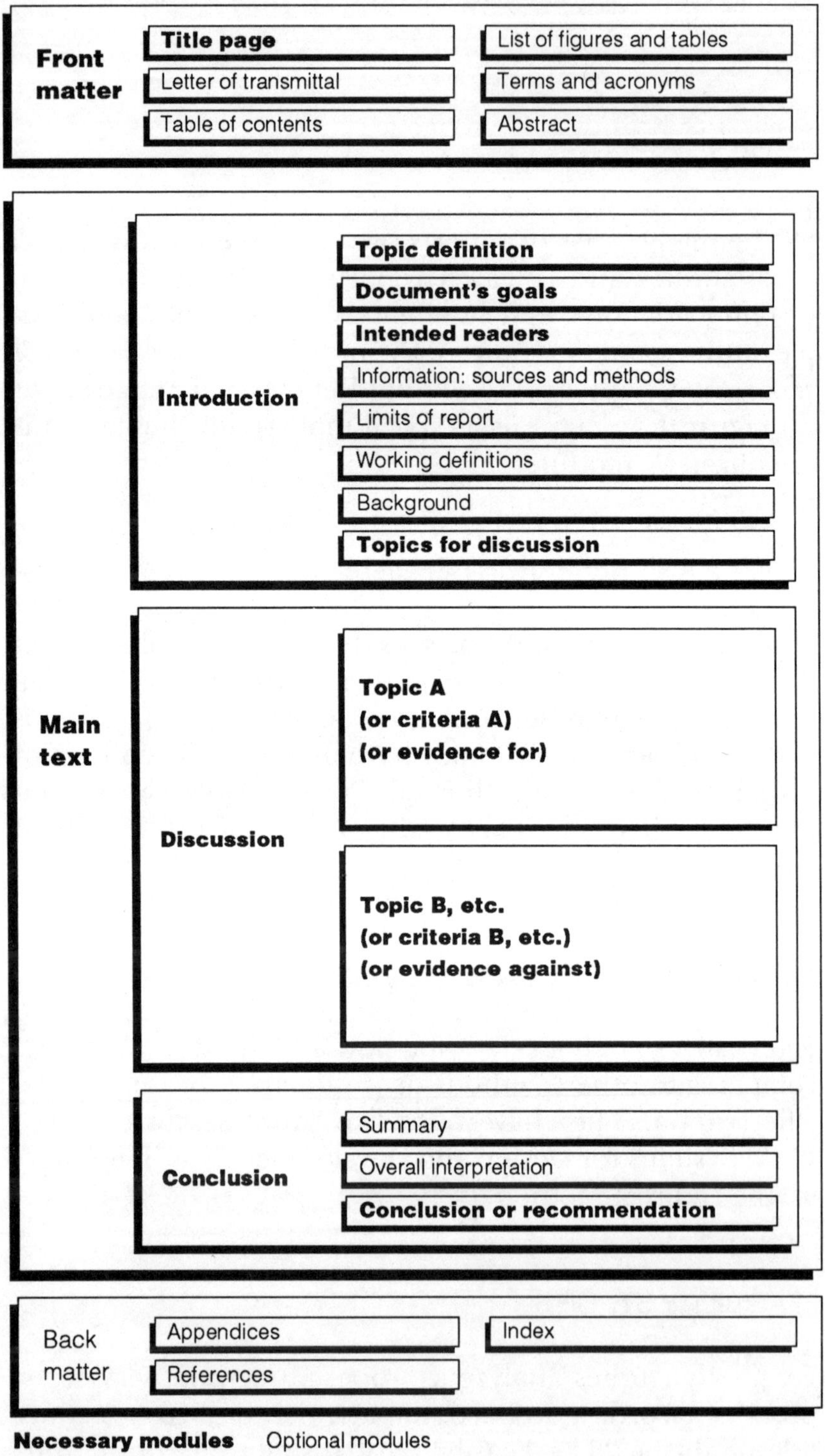

| Front matter | **Title page** | List of figures and tables |
| | Letter of transmittal | Terms and acronyms |
| | Table of contents | Abstract |

Main text

Introduction
- **Topic definition**
- **Document's goals**
- **Intended readers**
- Information: sources and methods
- Limits of report
- Working definitions
- Background
- **Topics for discussion**

Discussion

**Topic A
(or criteria A)
(or evidence for)**

**Topic B, etc.
(or criteria B, etc.)
(or evidence against)**

Conclusion
- Summary
- Overall interpretation
- **Conclusion or recommendation**

| Back matter | Appendices | Index |
| | References | |

**Necessary modules**   Optional modules

**Figure 1.4.** Modules in a Report.

RECOMMENDATIONS

Recommendations argue, logically, that benefits will result if someone adopts the recommendation's point of view or takes the action it proposes. These reports usually describe how to solve a problem or make improvements. Recommendations are actually a type of proposal, but we include them in this category because they are organized like reports. They have titles like "Why You Should Support the Smith-Weyman Proposal" or "How to Increase Profits by Adding Another Shift."

## MEMOS

The memo, the most common technical document, is often a short version of one of the other types of documents. We use them in the workplace every day to:

○ Report on a project's progress.

○ Propose a new project.

○ Propose changes for a procedure or equipment.

○ Report estimated costs for a new project.

○ Justify the results of an assignment.

○ Explain the reasons for a project's failure.

○ Report on a meeting or conference.

○ Request assistance.

Some organizations have a standard format for memos. A typical format is made up of modules like those in Figure 1.5.

Chapter 6, "Outlining Reports and Memos," describes memos in more detail and includes a sample outline.

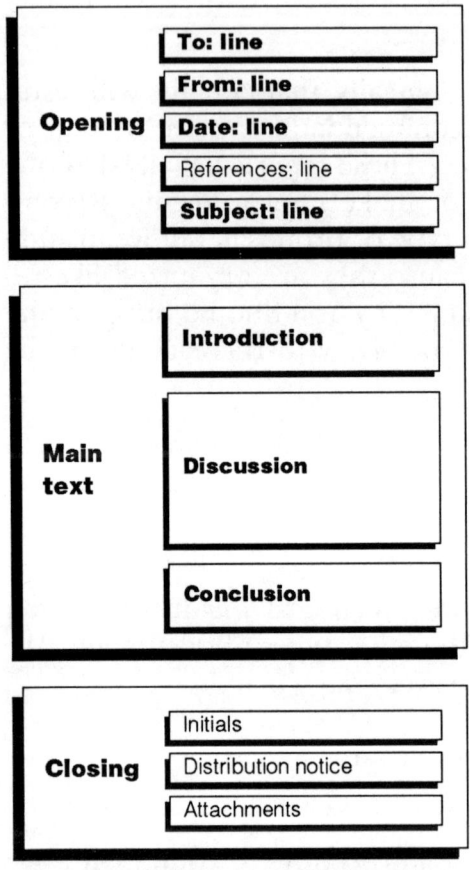

**Necessary modules**    Optional modules

**Figure 1.5.** Modules in a Memo.

## INSTRUCTIONAL MATERIALS

Instructional materials include all kinds of instructions and directions for use, such as user's manuals ("How to Operate and Maintain a Drill Press" or "How to Write a COBOL Program"), and procedures ("Configuration Management Procedures" or "Procedures for Rotating Personnel").

The way you organize instructional materials depends on who your readers will be, their needs, and your objectives. Generally, instructional materials include the modules diagrammed in Figure 1.6.

Chapter 7, "Outlining Instructional Materials," discusses instructional materials in detail and shows a sample outline.

## PROPOSALS

Proposals detail how a need will be met. They fall into two categories:

1. Offers of a service or product. (Our service or product will meet your needs and here's how and why.)

2. Requests for grants or research funds. (We deserve your support because our project is worthwhile and our qualifications guarantee its success.)

Businesses as well as private and government agencies usually have their own guidelines for preparing proposals. Generally, proposals for work contracts or grants include the modules diagrammed in Figure 1.7.

Chapter 8, "Outlining Proposals and Promotional Materials," discusses proposals in more detail and includes a sample outline.

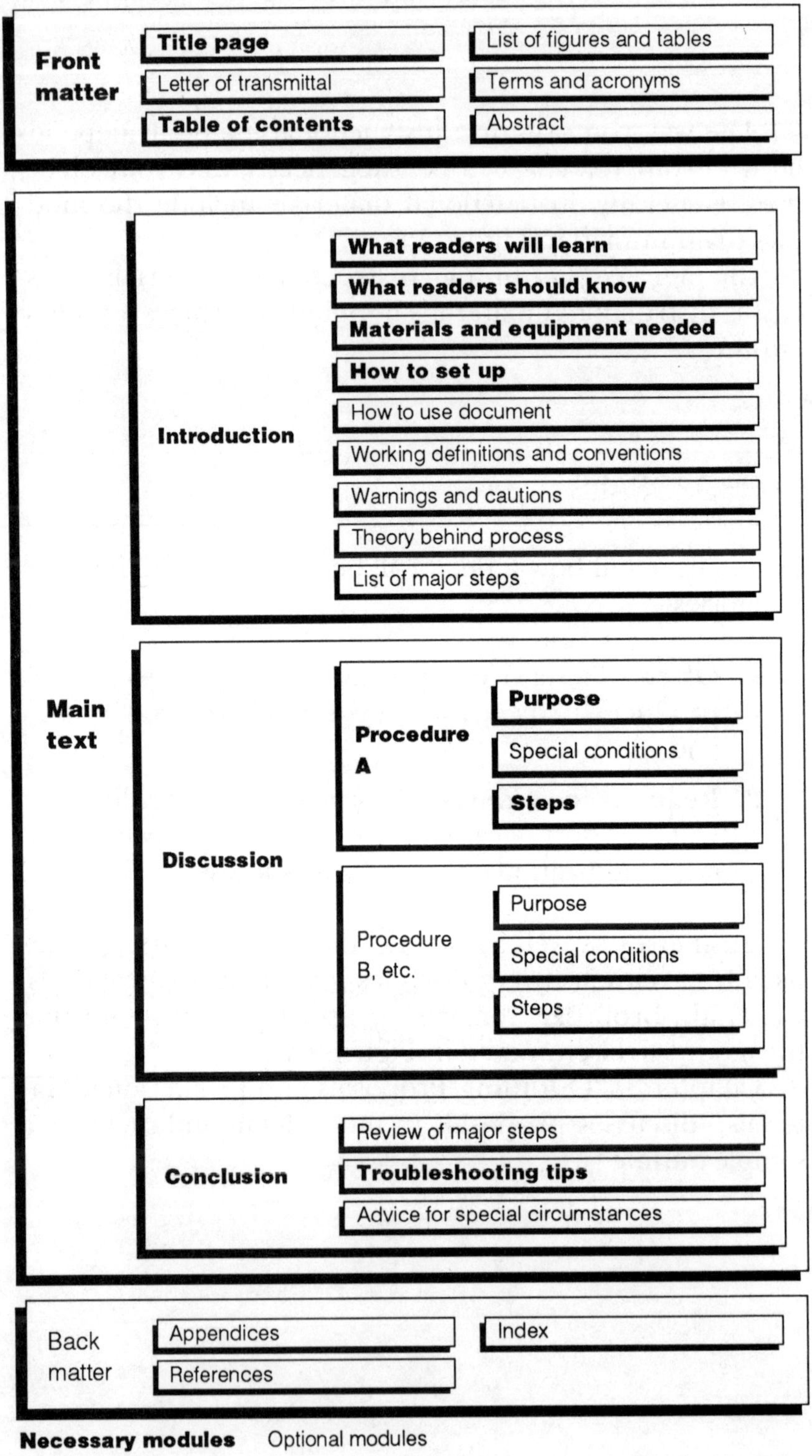

| Front matter | | |
|---|---|---|
| **Title page** | | List of figures and tables |
| Letter of transmittal | | Terms and acronyms |
| **Table of contents** | | Abstract |

**Main text**

**Introduction**
- **What readers will learn**
- **What readers should know**
- **Materials and equipment needed**
- **How to set up**
- How to use document
- Working definitions and conventions
- Warnings and cautions
- Theory behind process
- List of major steps

**Discussion**

Procedure A
- **Purpose**
- Special conditions
- **Steps**

Procedure B, etc.
- Purpose
- Special conditions
- Steps

**Conclusion**
- Review of major steps
- **Troubleshooting tips**
- Advice for special circumstances

| Back matter | | |
|---|---|---|
| Appendices | | Index |
| References | | |

**Necessary modules**    Optional modules

**Figure 1.6.** Modules in Instructional Material.

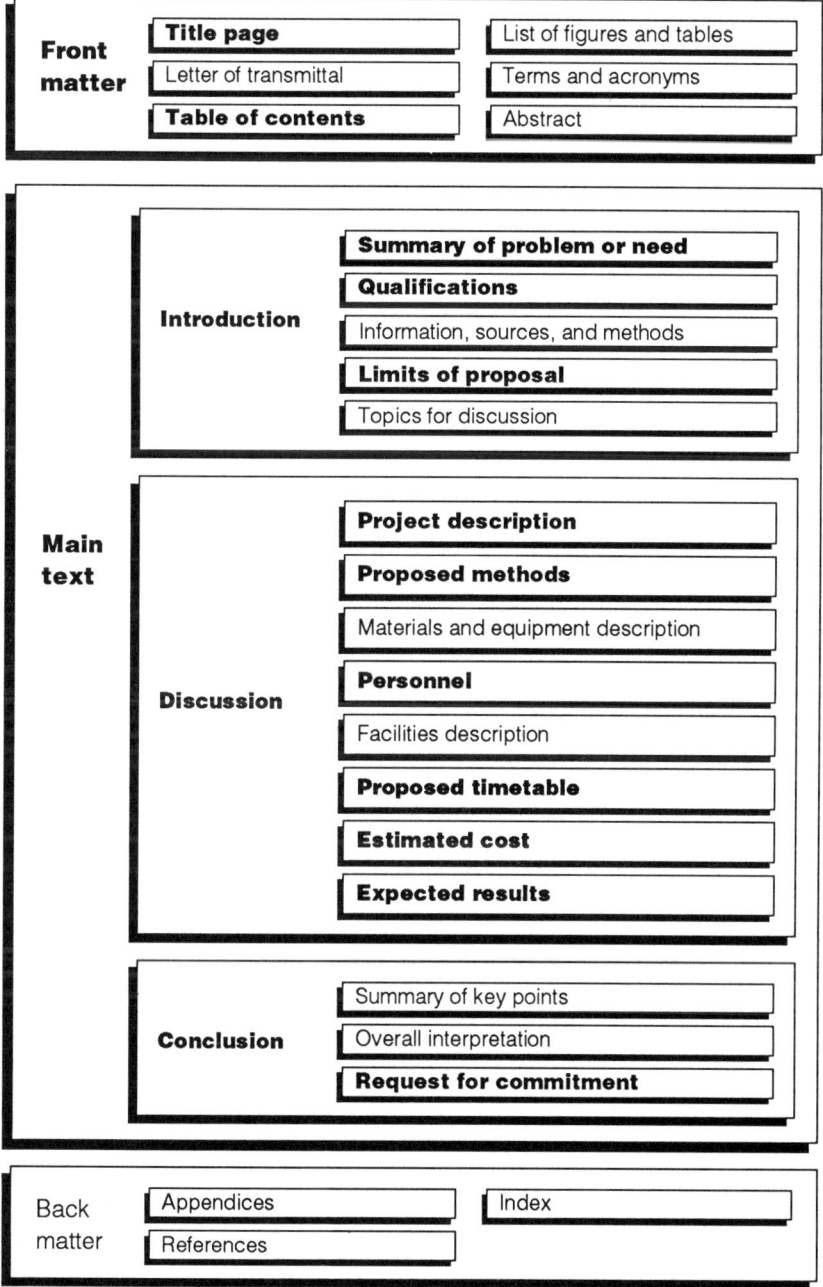

**Figure 1.7.** Modules in a Proposal.

## PROMOTIONAL MATERIALS

Brochures, direct mail pamphlets, advertisements, or articles for journals are types of promotional materials. They use persuasive strategies to convince people to buy a product or use a service.

Promotional materials generally contain the modules illustrated in Figure 1.8. See Chapter 8 for sample outlines and various approaches to organization.

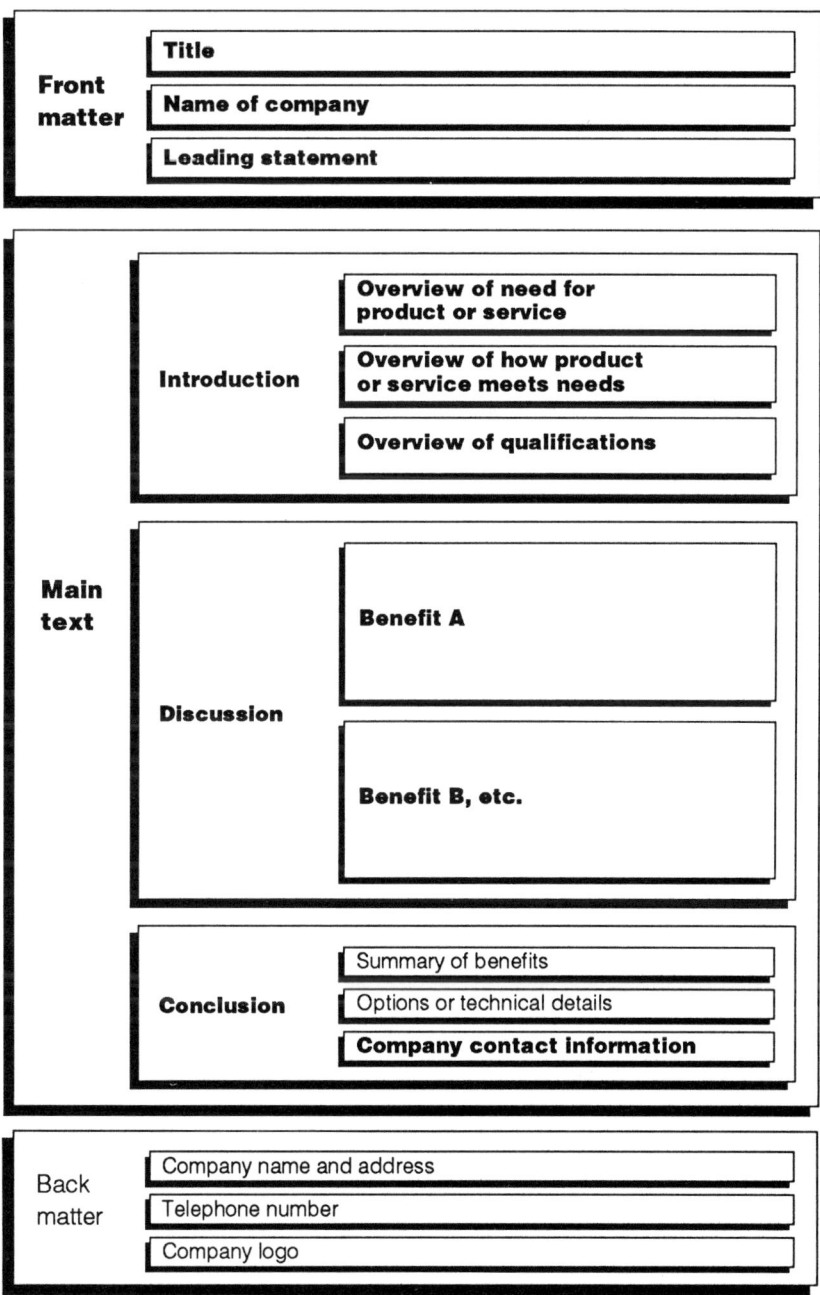

**Figure 1.8.** Modules in Promotional Material.

# CHAPTER 2

# Laying the Groundwork

THE WRITING PROCESS

CREATING A DOCUMENT PLAN

MAKING A SCHEDULE

—Do you know what steps are involved in creating your document?

—Do you know where to find existing information that can help you write it?

—Can you pinpoint the goals of your document?

—Who are your readers? What do they need from the document?

—How will you create the illustrations you need?

—Do you have layout guidelines for the pages or a design for the document?

—How will you reproduce or print copies?

—Who is responsible for the different tasks necessary in creating the document?

—Do you know how to create a realistic and workable schedule?

Have you ever reached the halfway point in a project only to be told that you're headed in the wrong direction? Unfortunately, we've all participated in projects that got off the track or were misdirected. Poor planning is usually the culprit.

This chapter covers planning in detail. We give an overview of the steps involved in the writing process, then describe how to create a workable document plan. We also include some pointers on making a realistic schedule.

## THE WRITING PROCESS

When your writing project is simple—writing a memo, for instance—the writing process may include only a few steps. You:

○  Jot down a few notes.

○  Write the memo.

○  Read and correct it.

○  Get a supervisor's approval, if necessary.

○  Have the memo copied and distributed.

When your writing project is more complex, the number of steps increases in proportion to the length and complexity of the document, the number of people involved, the extent of your responsibilities, and the sophistication of your production methods.

A writer's responsibilities can vary greatly, too. You may be responsible only for writing, or for both writing and editing. Or the entire project may be your responsibility, including writing, editing, and producing the document.

Figure 2.1 illustrates a typical process in planning, writing, and producing a complex document.

To help in your planning and scheduling, we've listed the major steps for the document plan, outline, the first and subsequent drafts, the final draft, the production phase, and binding, assembly, and distribution. These lists are overviews—the actual steps you take and the order in which you take them may vary for each project.

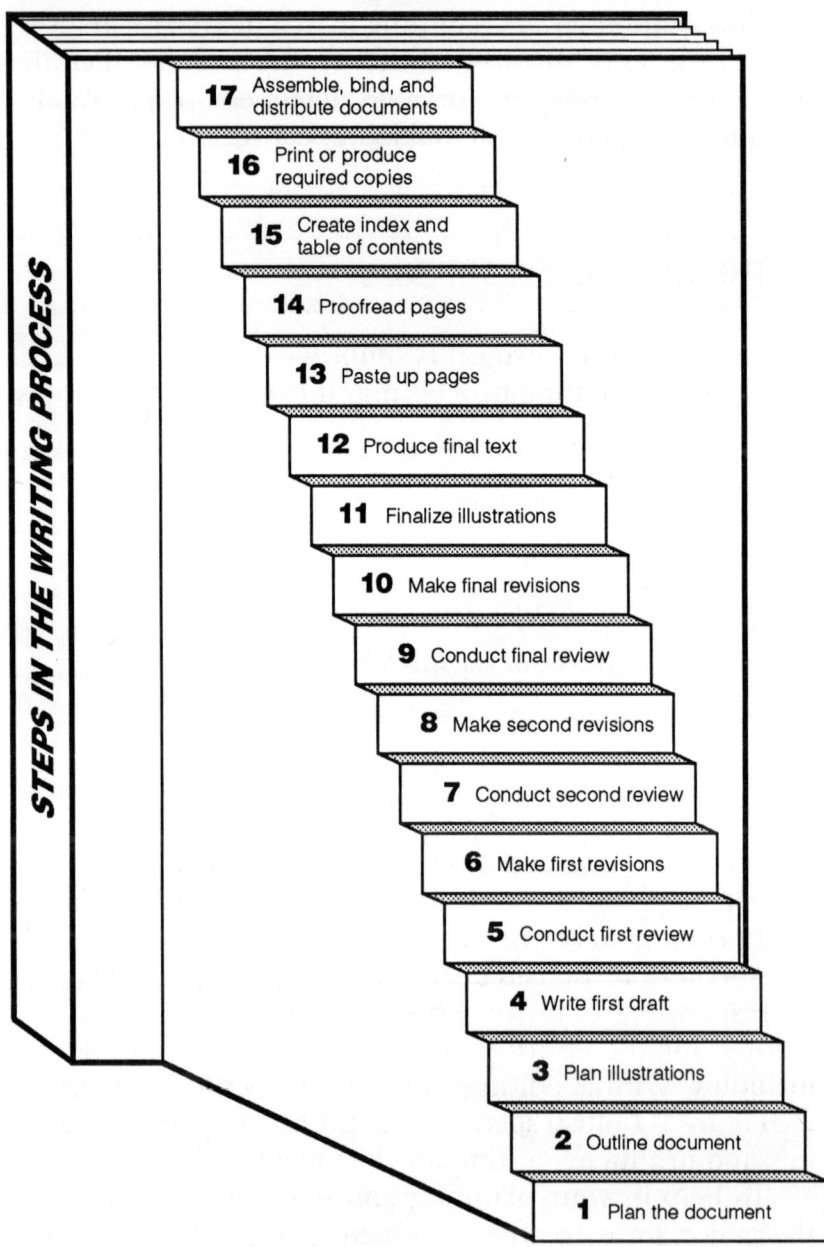

**Figure 2.1.** Steps in the Writing Process.

## DOCUMENT PLAN

1. Locate and review any existing information and confer with any other team members.

2. Decide on the goals of the document.

3. Write a profile of the readers.

4. Determine production methods, including the means for creating illustrations, producing a final draft, and reproducing or printing the required number of copies.

5. Describe the physical appearance of the document, its length, size, binding, etc.

6. Write a document plan and get it approved.

7. Draft a schedule and get it approved.

8. Create a style guide.

## OUTLINE

1. Review the information in your document plan about the readers and their needs and the document's goals.

2. Determine the type of document you need and which modules it should contain.

3. Decide which logical order is appropriate for each module.

4. Determine the points you need to make to accomplish your goals.

5. Draft a preliminary or working outline.

6. Review the outline and revise it if necessary.

7. Get the outline approved.

## FIRST DRAFT

1. Make a preliminary list of illustrations based on your outline.
2. Write the first draft.
3. Read and revise it.
4. Update the list of illustrations.
5. Send the draft out for review.

## SECOND DRAFT

Repeat for subsequent drafts as needed:

1. Incorporate comments and corrections from the review.
2. Do any necessary rewriting.
3. Make copies of completed illustrations and insert them in the draft.
4. Proofread and correct the draft, including both text and illustrations.
5. Send the draft out for review.

## FINAL DRAFT

1. Incorporate comments and corrections from the review.
2. Read all text and illustrations, checking for flow, clarity, and completeness.
3. Get final okays on changes from reviewers or supervisor.

4. Check text and illustrations for consistency and proofread for typographical, spelling, or placement errors.

5. Indicate spaces for illustrations and mark headings, words or phrases that need special emphasis, and page breaks, if necessary.

## PRODUCTION

1. Produce the text by typewriter, word processor, or computerized typesetting.

2. Proofread the text (or galleys, if document is professionally typeset).

3. Paste up pages, including illustrations.

4. Check for continuity and positioning of illustrations.

5. Number the pages of the document.

6. Prepare the table of contents and index.

7. Proofread page numbers for the index and table of contents.

8. If the document is to be reproduced on a printing press, check the blueline (sample of printed document) for accuracy, consistency, and placement of text on pages.

9. Print or duplicate required number of copies.

ASSEMBLY, BINDING, AND DISTRIBUTION

1. Collate and assemble the required number of copies of the document.

2. Add bindings or covers.

3. Distribute the copies.

## CREATING A DOCUMENT PLAN

Whether your document is long or short, simple or complex, you can save yourself a lot of time, frustration, and money by creating a *document plan* before you begin to write. A document plan includes the following:

○ A list of where to find existing information that can help you write your document.

○ A definition of the document's goals.

○ A profile (description) of the readers.

○ Specifications that describe the document's design (page layout, binding, etc.) and how the document will be produced.

○ A list of the people who will work on the document and their tasks.

The amount of detail you need to include in a document plan depends on the complexity of your document. When your document is simple, the document plan can be short and informal. For example, for a memo or short report, you might need to jot down only a few notes as reminders.

When your document is more complex, the document plan will be longer, more formal, and will include more detailed information.

At the end of this section you'll find two sample document plans: an informal document plan for a short informative report and a formal plan for a more complex recommendation report.

## LOCATING EXISTING INFORMATION

Often, when you are writing a document, you don't have to start from scratch. Information that can help you probably exists in a variety of forms. The following types of written materials, when they are available, can give you a good start.

- Project or document specifications
- Requirements definitions
- Design analyses
- Previous published versions of the document
- Previous drafts of the document completed by other writers
- Notes made by someone who has worked or is working on the project
- Records and statistics

People are resources too. A list of individuals who might have helpful information could include:

- Your supervisor (or the person who gave you the assignment)
- Specialists in the field or subject
- Writers who have worked on similar documents on the same subject

Information may exist in other media, such as:

○ Tapes

○ Films

○ Audio-visual presentations

○ On-line computer files

○ Computer diskettes

Let's say you are writing a short report summarizing the results of a study. Your resources would be the study itself and, if available, the person who conducted the study.

Or perhaps you're writing a user's guide for a software application. Your information list might include a previous version of the user's guide, notes kept by the present computer operator, a program specification, and information from the marketing department. And you would add the people themselves—the operator, the programmer who created the application, and the person in charge of marketing it.

For a more complex report, say a recommendation that your company switch from a manual drafting system to a CAD/CAM system, your information list would be longer and might look like this:

○ Brochures and cost estimates from CAD/CAM manufacturers

○ Last year's monthly schedules from drafting department

○ Installation time estimates from computer center supervisor

○ Training time estimates from drafting supervisor

○ Transcripts of telephone interviews with drafting supervisors from other companies participating in the project

Listing information sources helps locate information necessary to write the document. And your list may grow as you begin contacting the sources. The list itself serves as a handy reference in case anyone wants to know where you got your information.

Later, when you organize and outline the document, you'll refer to the goals in the document plan, see that you need to include information that will bring the managers around to your point of view, and see that you need to use persuasive tactics to move the board to action.

## DEFINING THE DOCUMENT'S GOALS

As part of your document plan, you need to define the document's goals, as you understand them. For instance, in planning a user's guide, you know you want to teach your readers how to use something, but do you want to teach them enough to make them experts or do you want to teach only the basics? Or, do you want to make them expert in only a few of the functions? The planning stage is the time to pinpoint exactly what you want the document to accomplish.

After you define the goals, go over them with anyone whose input may be critical. Before you begin to write, be sure that you're going in the right direction.

In a simple document, such as a progress report, your goal may be obvious. For instance, you might need to make a note reminding yourself that the manager needs to know whether the project is on schedule and that the supervisor needs to know about any potential problems that might affect the schedule.

In a more complex report, such as the recommendation for the CAD/CAM system we mentioned previously, the goal may also be obvious, but more complicated. For instance, here are the goals for that document:

○ Convince the managers that we could be more productive if we switched to a new CAD/CAM system.

○ Persuade the board of directors to approve the expenditure for the new system.

In this case, the broad goal is to get the company to purchase a new CAD/CAM system. To accomplish this, you define two subgoals: convince the managers that the purchase is beneficial and persuade the board members to approve the expenditure.

## WRITING A READERS PROFILE

A *readers profile* is a description of the readers that will not only help you decide how to organize the document but will also help you decide what style and tone of language to use. To create a readers profile:

○ Identify the group or groups of readers who will read your document.

○ Write descriptions of each group.

○ If you have more than one group of readers, decide which are primary readers and which are secondary.

In an informal document plan for something like a short report, creating a readers profile may take only a minute or two; you know exactly who your readers are. For instance, for a report summarizing the results of a conference attended by people in your department, you know what tone to use, how much technical detail to include, and what your readers need to know about the subject.

In a formal document plan for a more complicated document, such as a lengthy research report or a user's guide that has to serve a variety of groups, you have to analyze your readers before you can create a readers profile.

IDENTIFYING THE READERS.   If you know your readers belong to a single group of people with similar needs and similar backgrounds, identifying them is simple. They might be company managers, members of a profession, or operators of some piece of equipment.

However, when a document will have a large readership that includes different and varied groups, identifying your readers is more complicated. For instance, a document for company employees may include everyone from the warehouse workers to the executives to the board of directors, all with different needs and backgrounds.

Usually, you know who your readers are right from the beginning; they're tied in with the goals. But occasionally, you may have to look at the goals and then decide just who should read your document. For instance, if your organization wants you to write a report that will gain acceptance for a groundbreaking new system they have developed, you know you'll send it to your customers. But who else do you have to influence or convince to gain acceptance? Your competitors? A trade association? Workers in the field? A regulatory board? Stockholders? When you must choose the audience, first analyze the document's goals and then decide how you can accomplish them.

DESCRIBING THE READERS. To describe your readers, include any information that may affect their response to your document, such as:

- ○ Profession
- ○ Position in organization or field
- ○ Level of education
- ○ Age group
- ○ Knowledge about the field and the subject

You can also add to your readers profile by asking yourself these questions: To accomplish the document's goals, what do readers need to know about the subject? What might their attitudes be about the subject? Are they neutral? Curious? Supportive? Antagonistic? Defensive?

This information helps determine what information to include when you're outlining the document and what kind of language and tone to use when you're writing it.

As an example, let's return to our recommendation for the CAD/CAM system. The readers profile might look like this:

**Readers Profile**

Group 1: Company managers.

Group 2: Board of directors.

Both groups well educated, age group 45–62, primarily conservative.

Company managers
Managers must approve purchase of the new system and schedule installation and training time. They understand current drafting process, have overview of scope of defense project we're undertaking, and understand CAD/CAM systems. May not realize how we could benefit. Strong interest in improving productivity, but may be reluctant to approve the installation and training time necessary to switch to a new system.

Board of directors
Members of the board have to approve expenditure. They
understand current manual drafting system in general; don't
know details of process. Probably don't know much about a CAD/
CAM system or its benefits, but understand scope of defense
project, in general. Reluctant to approve large expenditures
for new equipment unless certain equipment will improve
productivity or sales. Usually follow managers'
recommendations.

For the outlining stage, this readers profile indicates
that you need to include strong evidence about the benefits
of the new CAD/CAM system for both groups. But you also
need to include a description of the current drafting system
so that board members can compare it with the proposed
system and see the potential for increased benefits.

For the writing stage, the profile tells you that you need
to adopt a respectful, businesslike tone to reach both of
these groups.

DECIDING ON PRIMARY AND SECONDARY READERS.    If you
have more than one group of readers, you need to decide
which groups are primary and which are secondary.

Often the primary readers are primary simply because
they make up a majority. Sometimes, however, the primary
group is fewer in number but more important in accomplishing your goals. For instance, you might write a report
directed to all company employees. The top executive officers need your document to make a decision; the rest of the
employees only need to be informed. The top executive
officers, although fewer in number, are your primary readers; the others are your secondary readers.

In the CAD/CAM system example, the managers are
the primary readers, not only because they are the majority,
but because their opinion counts most in accomplishing the
primary goal.

Occasionally, after you finish your readers profile, you'll find that you can't meet the needs of all readers and accomplish your goals with a single document. You may then have to consider writing two or more documents, each one slanted toward a different group of readers. You can see why taking a little care in this part of your planning is important.

## INCLUDING A DOCUMENT SPECIFICATION

Another part of your document plan is a *document specification*, a detailed description of your document's design that includes page size, page layout (margins, line spacing, indentations, etc.), and binding. The description also details how the document will be printed or reproduced, who will do the paste-up, what kind of illustrations it will contain, and how the illustrations will be produced.

You need this information for several reasons. It helps you prepare a realistic schedule, and it helps you make writing decisions. For instance, when a document needs a lot of time for production, the length of time allotted to writing may have to be shortened. You also need to know what type of illustrations to include and how many. If you have to dig up your own illustrations, photocopy them, and paste them on pages, for example, you need to make preparations and schedule your time accordingly. And, when your responsibilities include production, you need to determine who's responsible for each of the tasks involved.

Many organizations have standard specifications for the design of their documents. If your organization has a document specification available, you should either get a copy to include in your document plan or note where and from whom you can get this information.

But quite often, a writer's responsibilities include document design as well as writing. If you have to design your document, see the section on design in Chapter 3, "Planning Illustrations and Document Design."

AN INFORMAL DOCUMENT SPECIFICATION.   Your document may be simple and the specifications informal, perhaps consisting only of an example of the company's format and a note to schedule time for word processing, photocopying, and assembling.

A document specification may include more than a reminder or two but still fall short of the formal, detailed specification needed for a document that will be printed and bound. For instance, the specification might be a brief description covering:

○ Estimated length

○ Number of copies needed

○ Format for headings and words that need special emphasis

○ Type of illustrations

○ Names of people who will produce final copies (typists, word processors, photocopiers, and so on)

You can see examples of informal document specifications in the sample document plans near the end of this section.

A FORMAL DOCUMENT SPECIFICATION.   A formal document specification answers some or all of the following questions about how the document will be produced.

○ Will the document be typewritten? Word processed? Typeset? Printed in-house or by an outside printing company?

○ Will the illustrations be produced by graphic artists? With CAD/CAM equipment? Photocopied from other sources for pasting in?

○ How will the paste-up, if any, be accomplished? By the writer? By paste-up artists? On desktop publishing equipment?

○ How will the document be collated, assembled, and bound? By the writer? By clerical help? By a printer or binding company?

A formal document specification also describes such design and production details as:

○ Number of copies needed

○ Estimate of the final page count

○ Size of page (a standard 8½ × 11 inches or larger or smaller)

○ Binding (three-ring binder, spiral binding, or brad-type binding)

○ Printed one side of the paper or both sides

○ Illustrations (line drawings, photographs, charts, tables, screen dumps, or photocopies from various sources)

○ Page layout (including margins, line spacing, type size for text and various headings, type for special emphasis, and the format for footers, headers, and footnotes)

Specifications can also include descriptions of the paper to be used, information on inks, and other printing details. Pay particular attention to elements that can help you influence readers, such as the use of additional colors, screening, and multiple columns.

## LISTING THE PEOPLE INVOLVED

A document plan should also include a list of the people involved in the project, their responsibilities, and how to contact them. These people might include:

○ Project supervisors

○ Other people whose approvals are needed

○ Other writers

○ Editors

○ Reviewers

○ Proofreaders

○ Typists, word processors, or typesetter

○ Photocopy personnel

○ Illustrators

○ Paste-up artists

○ Graphic artists and illustrators

○ Printers

○ Assembly and binding personnel

○ Distribution personnel

This list will help you coordinate your part of the project, schedule your time, and make sure that the document gets to the right people on time.

## SAMPLE DOCUMENT PLANS

We show two examples of document plans here, an informal one for a memo and a more formal one for the CAD/CAM recommendation discussed earlier.

AN INFORMAL DOCUMENT PLAN.   This memo summarizes information for the busy executives of a company that manufactures solar heating panels. The document plan consists of notes jotted down on a single sheet of paper that the writer has stapled inside the front cover of the file folder for this project.

**Subject**
Development of new technology for solar heating by Ceede Sun Labs.

**Sources of Information**

○ Article in February issue of the *Journal*.

○ "Proceedings" from Solar Heating Conference.

○ Jim Gray, KRC Co., who attended conference and sent me a copy of the "Proceedings."

**Reader Profile**

○ Primary readers—upper-level managers. Know about solar heating, our solar panels, and recent trends.

○ Secondary readers—lower-level managers. Know about solar heating and solar panels, but perhaps not aware of recent trends.

**Goals**
To make management aware of the recent developments in solar heating technology by Ceede Sun Labs that may affect our firm's plans.

**Document Specs**

○ About 10 pages long.

○ 35 copies.

○ Standard memo format.

○ Will photocopy illustrations from article and the "Proceedings" document.

○ Word processing department will produce.

○ Copy center will copy and assemble.

○ Department secretary will distribute.

**List of People Involved**
Karla Long, Department Manager, Ext. 322
Betty Green, Word Processing, Ext. 423
C. D. Long, Copy Center, Ext. 401
Jim Gray (will review), 206/328-8811

A FORMAL DOCUMENT PLAN.   This plan is for the CAD/ CAM recommendation previously discussed.

### Subject
Recommendation for new CAD/CAM system.

### Goals

- O To convince management of the benefits of switching from our current manual drafting system to a new CAD/ CAM system.
- O To persuade board of directors to approve expenditure.

### Readers Profile
Company managers and board of directors.

Both groups well educated, age group 45–62, primarily conservative and male.

Company managers—primary audience. Need their approval. They schedule installation and training time. Understand current drafting process, have overview of scope of defense project we are undertaking. Also understand CAD/CAM systems, but may not understand how we could benefit from one. Strong interest in improving productivity, but may be reluctant to approve the installation and training time necessary to switch to a new system.

Board of directors—secondary audience. Need their approval for expenditure. Generally understand current manual drafting system; don't know details of process. Probably don't know much about a CAD/CAM system or its benefits. Generally understand scope of defense project. Reluctant to approve large expenditures for new equipment unless certain it will improve productivity or sales. Usually follow recommendations of managers.

### Sources of Information

- O Brochures and cost estimates from CAD/CAM representative.
- O Last year's monthly schedules from drafting department.
- O Installation time estimates from Ruby Gardner.
- O Training time estimates from J. Angus.
- O Transcripts of telephone interviews with drafting supervisors from other companies participating in the project.

### Document Specifications

Length: Approximately 60 pages

Number of copies: 75

Page size: 8-1/2 × 11 inches, printed one side

Cover: 1/2-inch wide gray 3-ring binders, stick-on labels with title and company logo

Illustrations: Samples of blueprints produced by our system and by proposed system; charts produced with our computers and printed with our laser printers.

Layout: Production department specs attached. (Can use multiple columns, tables.)

Production: Offset printing, PrintPro Press

Assembly and binding: PrintPro

### Personnel

Writer: Jan Foster

Manager: C. Lupone, Ext. 211

Editor: Marie Fuqua, Ext. 225

Technical reviewer: F. D. Long, Ext. 227

Production Supervisor: Jeanine Geffs, Ext. 422

Word processing department (final copy), Ext. 531

Computer Center Supervisor: Ruby Gardner, Ext. 473

Drafting Supervisor: J. Angus, Ext. 365

CAD/CAM Representative: M. J. McCollum, Ext. 278

Mail room (distribution): Ext. 344

Printing and Assembly: PrintPro Printers, J. Barlow, 433-2652

Some writers include a schedule in their document plan. Because of its special importance in creating technical documents, we're discussing it as a separate subject.

## MAKING A SCHEDULE

The schedule is slipping again. Early in the project you tried to tell them that a second review would be necessary but they wouldn't listen. And now they're blaming you, the writer, because the document won't be finished on the due date.

Writers are often under a great deal of pressure to complete a document. Personnel in other departments may not realize how many steps go into creating a document or how much time certain processes—like editing and reviewing—can take. As a result, writers may end up working overtime to meet unrealistic deadlines. This section contains guidelines to help you avoid that stressful situation.

### CREATING A PRELIMINARY SCHEDULE

The complexity and length of your schedule depends on the complexity of the document and on how many other people are involved. The steps in the scheduling process usually go like this:

1. Pinpoint the delivery date and any midpoint dates.

2. List all of the steps involved in the process.

3. Get estimates on how long everyone will take to perform each of the necessary steps.

4. Map out the steps or events on a calendar.

5. If you can't meet the delivery date at this point, decide which tasks can be completed in less time than originally estimated.

6. Draft the schedule and get commitments.

7. Get the preliminary schedule approved.

First establish your deadlines, including the final delivery date and any due dates that come midway, such as delivery of a review draft or a handoff of the document to the production staff. Then list the steps necessary for completing the document. The description of the writing process at the beginning of this chapter can help you.

At this point, discuss the schedule with others involved in the project. Consult with editors, proofreaders, graphic artists, printers, and anyone else who is working on the document. For instance, if you need word processing support, talk to the word processing supervisor, describing the length of your document and any special formatting it requires. Find out when that department can schedule your project and how long it will take.

After you get estimates on how long each step will take, begin making your preliminary schedule. Using a calendar, map out the major steps. Count only work days and be sure the major events don't conflict with vacations, holidays, or the schedules of other on-going projects. Plan for a reasonable number of hours per day for your document, taking into consideration other projects you are working on, time for meetings, and so forth. Don't underestimate the editing and review process; you want to be certain all your material is accurate and well written.

You may find that you can't meet the proposed deadline. In that case, you have some negotiating to do. The information you've gathered in creating this preliminary schedule can back up your arguments for a more realistic deadline. If the deadline is nonnegotiable, you'll have to consider cutting time from various steps in the process, shrinking the scope of the project, or reducing the quality of the final document. Make sure that everyone involved agrees on these compromises at the outset. No one wants to be unpleasantly surprised at the end of the project.

When everyone involved is in agreement, write down the proposed schedule, specifying dates on which the other participants are expected to begin and complete their tasks. Give copies of the schedule to the participants and ask them to review it and commit to the scheduled dates.

## UPDATING THE SCHEDULE

Keep in mind that your first schedule will be a rough draft and that changes are inevitable. And when changes in the schedule are necessary, be sure to inform the others promptly.

If your project is complex, you may need to pick a project leader or a scheduler to keep track of the document's progress, update the schedule each week, and keep everyone informed of schedule changes.

## SAMPLE SCHEDULE

The following schedule is an example of one created for a fairly complex computer manual.

SCHEDULE

Project: ChArtist User's Manual
Project Manager: Joel Geffs
Scheduler: Jill Foster
Weekly meeting: Tuesday 9 a.m., Room 217

Preliminary Schedule

| | |
|---|---|
| January 13–15 | Review document plan and outline. |
| January 19–20 | Revise document plan and outline. |
| January 25–26 | Review final document plan and outline. |
| January 27 | Begin writing Part 1. Begin producing Part 1 illustrations. |

| | |
|---|---|
| February 29–<br>March 10 | Review Part 1. |
| March 14–17 | Revise Part 1. |
| March 21–23 | Final review of Part 1.<br>Begin writing Part 2.<br>Begin producing Part 2 illustrations. |
| April 18–25 | Review of Part 2. |
| April 25–<br>May 6 | Revise Part 2. |
| May 9–12 | Final review of Part 2. |
| May 9 | Begin writing appendices. |
| May 30–June 3 | Review appendices. |
| June 6–10 | Revise appendices. |
| June 13–14 | Final review of appendices. |
| June 15–30 | Final corrections. |
| July 4 | Hand off to production editor. |
| August 1 | Hand off to printer. |
| September 1 | Completed manual in warehouse. |

A document plan, whether an informal one consisting of a few notes for a short report, or a formal, multipage plan for a 550-page user's guide, saves time and effort and helps you create a document more likely to reach your goals. And by creating realistic and workable schedules, you can keep the process of producing a document running smoothly.

# CHAPTER 3

# Planning Illustrations and Document Design

TYPES OF ILLUSTRATIONS

PLANNING DOCUMENT DESIGN

—What kind of illustrations should you use in your document? Should you use diagrams? Charts and graphs? Tables?

—How will you bind your document?

—Do you have a design? Guidelines for page layout?

—How will you make your headings stand out as guideposts for your readers?

—How will you set off special terms and examples?

—How can you make lists and procedures easy to read?

—How should you handle running heads and running feet? Footnotes?

Have you ever had to assemble a piece of equipment when the instructions were nothing but page after page of solid text, with no illustrations whatsoever to help you out? Or how about that awful report you couldn't make any sense of because it had no headings and no charts?

Illustrations and page design are important to all types of documents. They help readers understand the text and follow the writer's train of thought.

As part of your document plan, you listed resources available for creating illustrations and for producing the document. With this information, you can plan the illustrations and, if necessary, the design of the document. You need to consider resources, cost, and schedule.

- O  Do you have the materials, equipment, and personnel necessary to produce the illustrations and the design?
- O  Will the cost of the illustrations and the design fall within your budget?
- O  Can you produce the illustrations and the design within the time available?

This chapter contains guidelines for planning the illustrations for your document and helpful suggestions for layout and design.

## TYPES OF ILLUSTRATIONS

Diagrams, graphs, charts, and tables help your readers understand the information in your document. They support and clarify your text, break up intimidating blocks of technical descriptions and explanations, and make your document more interesting.

## DIAGRAMS

You can use a diagram to show readers the steps in a procedure, the stages of a process, or to help them visualize objects, such as parts or mechanisms.

For instance, the diagram in Figure 3.1 is of a foundation wall, cut away to show how the floor joists sit on the wall. Like all good diagrams, this one is simple and uncluttered. The artist has eliminated all unnecessary detail.

Sometimes you need to illustrate a concept rather than a concrete detail. Figure 3.2 illustrates a technical concept, making it clearer than is possible with words alone.

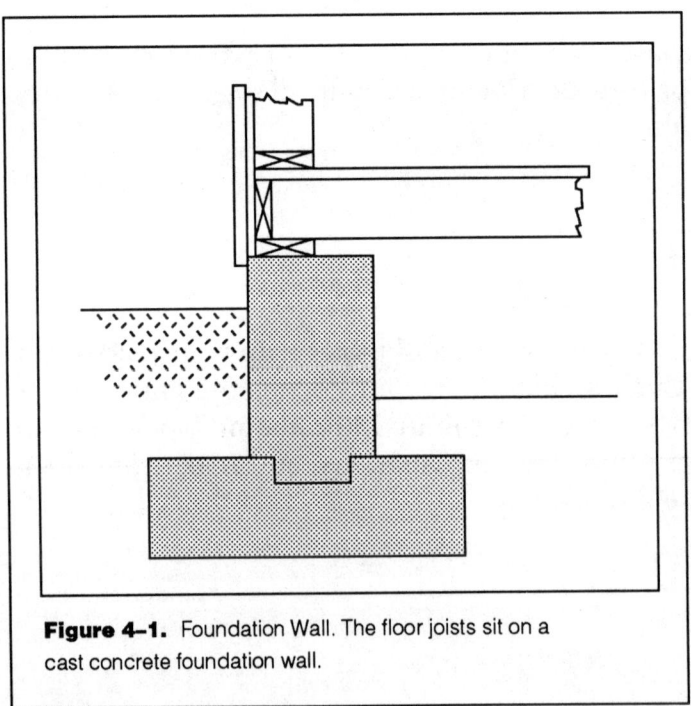

**Figure 4–1.** Foundation Wall. The floor joists sit on a cast concrete foundation wall.

**Figure 3.1.** Example of a Diagram.

**Figure 15.** Aggregate in the Dryer Operation. Fine aggregate holds more moisture than coarse aggregate, and so requires more heat for drying.

**Figure 3.2.** Example of a Diagram Illustrating a Concept.

## CHARTS

Charts present data graphically to readers, showing proportions and relationships in a way that text alone cannot.

Pie charts show the relative sizes of parts that make up a whole. For instance, you might use a pie chart to show how much of the total budget was spent proportionately on materials, labor, overhead, advertising, and so on. Or a pie chart could illustrate the relative proportions of the various causes of accidents in a factory.

Figure 3.3 shows data displayed first as text and then presented in a pie chart. You can see how effectively the chart supports the text, emphasizing the data in a dramatic way.

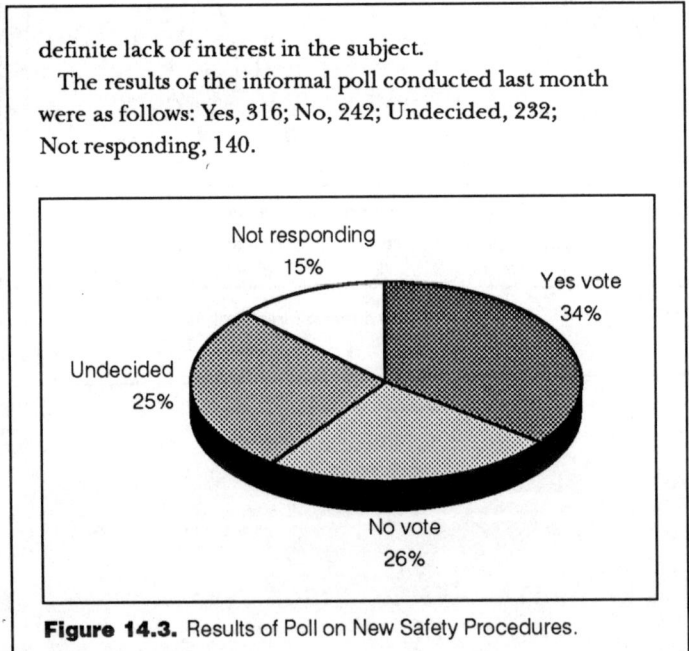

definite lack of interest in the subject.

The results of the informal poll conducted last month were as follows: Yes, 316; No, 242; Undecided, 232; Not responding, 140.

**Figure 14.3.** Results of Poll on New Safety Procedures.

**Figure 3.3.** Example of a Pie Chart.

The guidelines for creating a pie chart are:

○ Use between two and eight parts to make up the "pie."

○ Make sure the percentages add up to 100 percent.

○ Combine very small parts into one part labelled "Other."

○ Make your labels horizontal, when possible.

Some other common types of charts are:

*Organization charts*—show the levels of management and their relationships to each other.

*Flowcharts*—show the steps of a process from beginning to end.

*Tree charts*—show the relationships between the parts of an idea or a concept.

*Pictorial charts*—show numerical relationships and use symbols to depict specified quantities of the items.

## GRAPHS

You can use graphs to display, to make comparisons, to show changes over a period of time, or to illustrate trends. Choose either a line graph or a bar graph, depending on your needs.

LINE GRAPHS.   Line graphs, because they can have more data points than a bar graph, are good for presenting large amounts of information. Use a line graph to show trends and changes, such as how the profit-and-loss position has changed over the months or how the crusade against smoking has slowly lowered the incidence of lung cancer.

Figure 3.4 shows the flow of work orders in a manufacturing division over a twelve-month period.

The guidelines for creating a line graph are:

O  Avoid distorting the data to fit the graph.

O  Limit the number of lines on a graph to three.

O  Mark all of the data points on your lines.

O  Label each line clearly.

BAR GRAPHS.   You can use bar graphs to show differences in variables. For instance, you could use a bar graph to compare the population of several cities or to compare the company's net profit over the past several years.

Figure 3.5 shows production figures for a company that produces radon testing kits. Readers can interpret the chart at a glance and later, when they refer to the document again, easily locate this information.

The guidelines for creating a bar graph are:

O  Don't distort the data to fit the graph.

O  Keep the graph simple.

O  Use units of 1 or multiples of 2, 5, or 10 to number the scales.

O  Be sure to label both scales.

O  Use tick marks or grid lines to show the values.

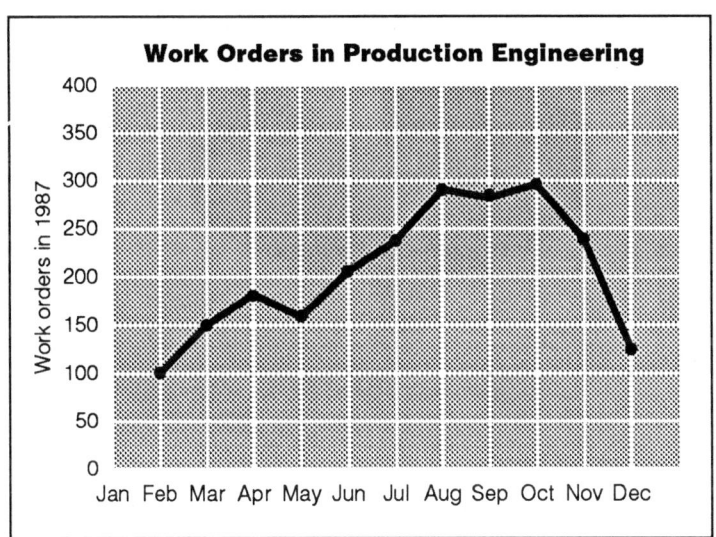

**Figure 3.4.** Example of a Line Graph.

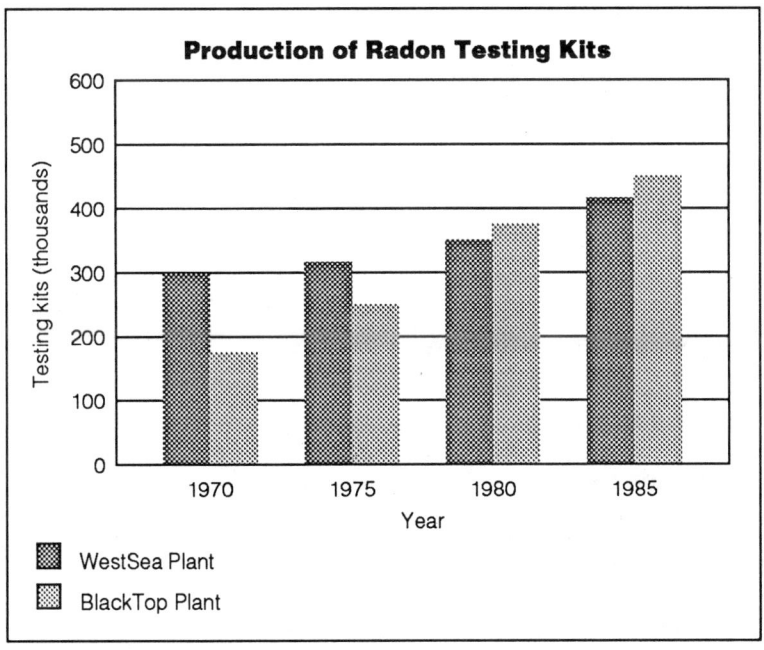

**Figure 3.5.** Example of a Bar Graph.

## TABLES

Tables are useful for displaying data in exact quantities or comparing large amounts of information. Figure 3.6 shows how data arranged in a table is much more readable than ordinary text.

The guidelines for creating a table are:

○ Keep it simple; don't have so many rows or columns that the table becomes hard to read.

○ Space the items for easy reading; avoid both crowding them and spacing them too far apart.

○ Use the vertical columns for your data, not the horizontal rows.

we want headers the right size.

For a 2x6 header, the maximum span is 3'6"; for a 2x8 header, 5'0"; for a 2x10 header, 6'6"; for a 2x12 header, 8'0".

Table 2.1 shows the maximum spans for headers.

**Table 2.1.** Maximum Spans for Headers.

| HEADER SIZE | MAXIMUM SPAN |
|---|---|
| 2x6 | 3'6' |
| 2x8 | 5'0' |
| 2x10 | 6'6' |
| 2x12 | 8'0' |

**Figure 3.6.** A Table Makes Data Stand Out.

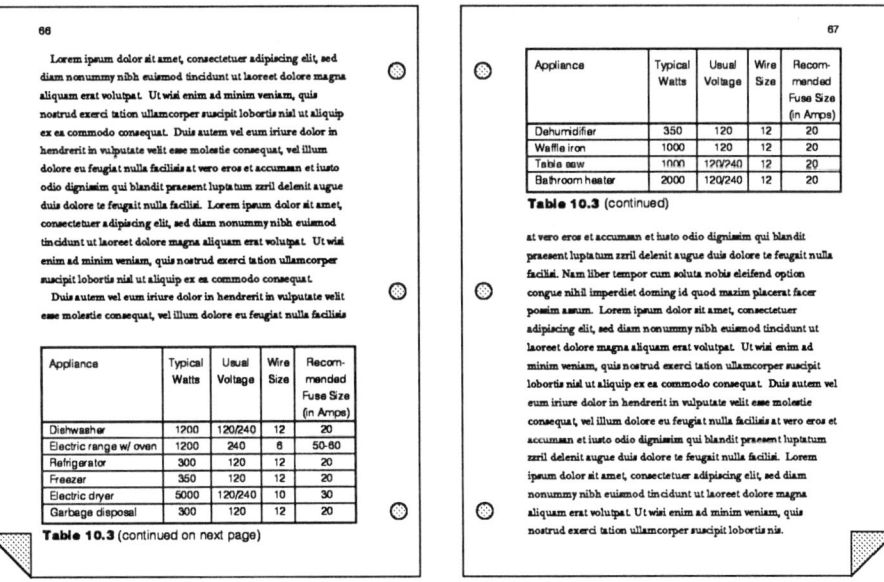

**Figure 3.7.** A Continued Table.

○ Label each column.

○ Try to keep the table on one page. If it's too big to fit on one page, divide the information into two or more tables. If you have to break a table between pages, be sure to repeat the column headings on the next page, as shown in Figure 3.7.

Often, you will have complex data to display in a table. Figure 3.8 illustrates the parts or format of a complex table.

Figure 3.9 is an example of complex data displayed in a table.

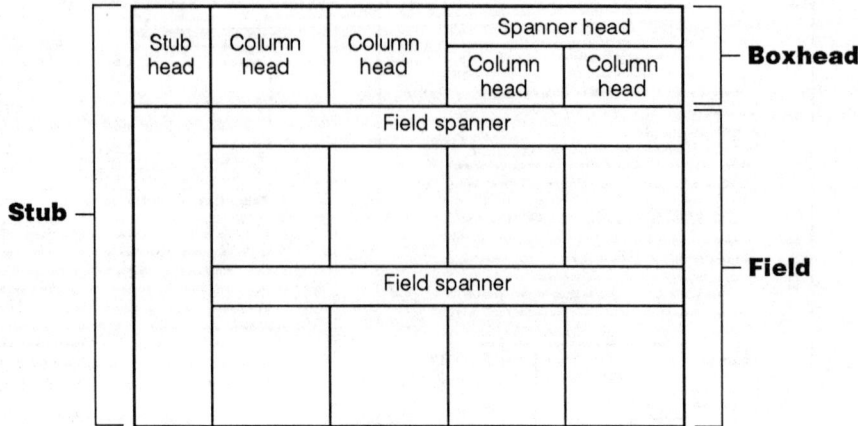

**Figure 3.8.**  Format for a Complex Table.

## CHOOSING ILLUSTRATIONS

Use as many diagrams, charts, graphs, and tables as you need to support your text. Good sources for illustration ideas are other documents. Look over documents similar to the one you're writing and decide which illustrations work and which merely fill up space.

Begin planning your illustrations early. You may need to plan for the services of artists, borrow equipment or find drawings in other documents to photocopy. To be sure everything will be ready when you need it, make your arrangements as soon as you can.

**Table 1.1.** Damper Specifications.

| Steel Dampers | | | | | |
|---|---|---|---|---|---|
| Width of Fireplace in Inches | Damper Dimensions in Inches | | | | |
| | A | B | C | D | E |
| 24 to 26 | 28 1/4 | 26 3/4 | 13 | 24 | 9 1/2 |
| 27 to 30 | 32 1/4 | 30 3/4 | 13 | 28 | 9 1/2 |
| 31 to 34 | 36 1/4 | 34 3/4 | 13 | 32 | 9 1/2 |
| 35 to 38 | 40 1/4 | 38 3/4 | 13 | 36 | 9 1/2 |
| 39 to 42 | 44 1/4 | 42 3/4 | 13 | 40 | 9 1/2 |
| 43 to 46 | 48 1/4 | 46 3/4 | 13 | 44 | 9 1/2 |
| 47 to 50 | 52 1/4 | 50 3/4 | 13 | 48 | 9 1/2 |
| 51 to 54 | 56 1/4 | 54 3/4 | 13 | 52 | 9 1/2 |
| 57 to 60 | 62 1/2 | 60 3/4 | 13 | 58 | 9 1/2 |
| Cast Iron Dampers | | | | | |
| Width of Fireplace in Inches | Damper Dimensions in Inches | | | | |
| | A | B | C | D | E |
| 24 to 26 | 28 | 21 | 13 1/2 | 24 | 10 |
| 27 to 30 | 34 | 26 3/4 | 13 1/2 | 30 | 10 |
| 31 to 34 | 37 | 29 3/4 | 13 1/2 | 33 | 10 |
| 35 to 38 | 40 | 32 3/4 | 13 1/2 | 36 | 10 |
| 39 to 42 | 46 | 38 3/4 | 13 1/2 | 48 | 10 |
| 43 to 46 | 52 | 44 3/4 | 13 1/2 | 48 | 10 |
| 47 to 50 | 57 1/2 | 50 1/2 | 13 1/2 | 54 | 10 |
| 51 to 54 | 64 | 56 1/2 | 13 1/2 | 60 | 11 1/2 |
| 57 to 60 | 76 | 58 | 13 1/2 | 72 | 11 1/2 |

**Figure 3.9.** Example of a Complex Table.

After you finish outlining your document and before you begin to write, go through your outline, locating and listing all of the information that an illustration could clarify. Describe the kind of illustration you need and how you will obtain it. For instance, you might write a document recommending that your organization install computer-aided-design equipment. Your list of illustrations could look like this:

   O  Example of design produced by CAD system. Ask CAD representative to provide.

   O  Diagram showing layout of present workroom. Artwork should already exist. Check with graphics department.

   O  Diagram showing layout of central computer room. Graphics department will render from my rough sketch.

Divide the illustrations in your list into two categories, essential and optional. Use your time and resources to produce the illustrations that are essential first. Then you can turn your attention to those that are optional.

When you write the first draft, you'll probably revise this list, changing some illustrations, adding or deleting others.

Follow the same procedure to make a separate list for tables.

## USING TITLES AND NUMBERS FOR ILLUSTRATIONS

If the illustrations in your document are few and far between and will be placed on the page right after you mention them, you probably don't need to label them. If, however, you're including numerous illustrations, refer to them by number or by both number and title. The general guidelines are:

- O  Number your illustrations and give them titles.

- O  If you have numerous illustrations, include a "List of Figures" (or "List of Tables") at the beginning of your document. (See the example in the sample document in Chapter 16.)

In a simple document, a simple numbering system (1, 2, 3, etc.) is fine. For a document divided into numbered sections or chapters, consider using a system that will help readers easily locate specific illustrations. For instance, you might number the illustrations for the first two chapters of a document like this:

        Figure 1.1.   A Sample Menu.
        Figure 1.2.   The Mouse.
        Figure 2.1.   Choosing a Command.
        Figure 2.2.   Filling in a Command Field.

## PLANNING DOCUMENT DESIGN

This section contains guidelines for designing documents. (Some printers and typesetters offer expert advice on layout and design, and for a major project, you might consider hiring the services of a graphic designer.)

Generally speaking, two of the most important elements in design are consistency and the use of *white space* (empty space). They make your document easier to read, more attractive, and more professional looking.

To achieve consistency, decide on the elements of your design and then stick to them. These elements, described in this chapter, include:

Line spacing, margins, and indentation

Headings

Illustrations

Lists and procedures

Emphasis of special text

Running heads and running feet

Footnotes

Binding

To make sure your document has enough white space:

○ Plan for adequate margins, indentations, and line spacing.

○ Arrange series of items into easy-to-follow lists.

○ Arrange procedures or descriptions of processes into procedure lists.

○ Begin the first page of a document or the first page of sections one-third of the way down the page.

For examples of how to design the tables of contents, abstracts, and indexes, see the sample documents in Chapter 16.

## LINE SPACING, MARGINS, AND INDENTATIONS

Double-space the text throughout the document. If you must limit the number of pages, you might use 1½ lines of spacing. (If your document will be professionally typeset or printed, these services can help you decide on line spacing.) To make it easier for readers to see where one paragraph ends and the next one begins, indent the first line of each paragraph. You can indent as many spaces as you wish— three and five spaces are the most common—as long as you're consistent.

If saving space is not a consideration and giving the document a lot of white space is, you can put three or four lines of spacing between paragraphs. When you do this, indenting the first line of your paragraphs isn't necessary.

On the title page, put four line spaces between the title and the beginning of the text.

Long lines of text are hard to read. Plan your margins so that the lines are between 50 and 60 characters per line. Generally, margins should be no smaller than these measurements:

Top margin, 1¼ inches

Bottom margin, 1½ inches

Right margin, 1¼ inches

Left margin, 2 inches

Figure 3.10 shows a typical page layout.

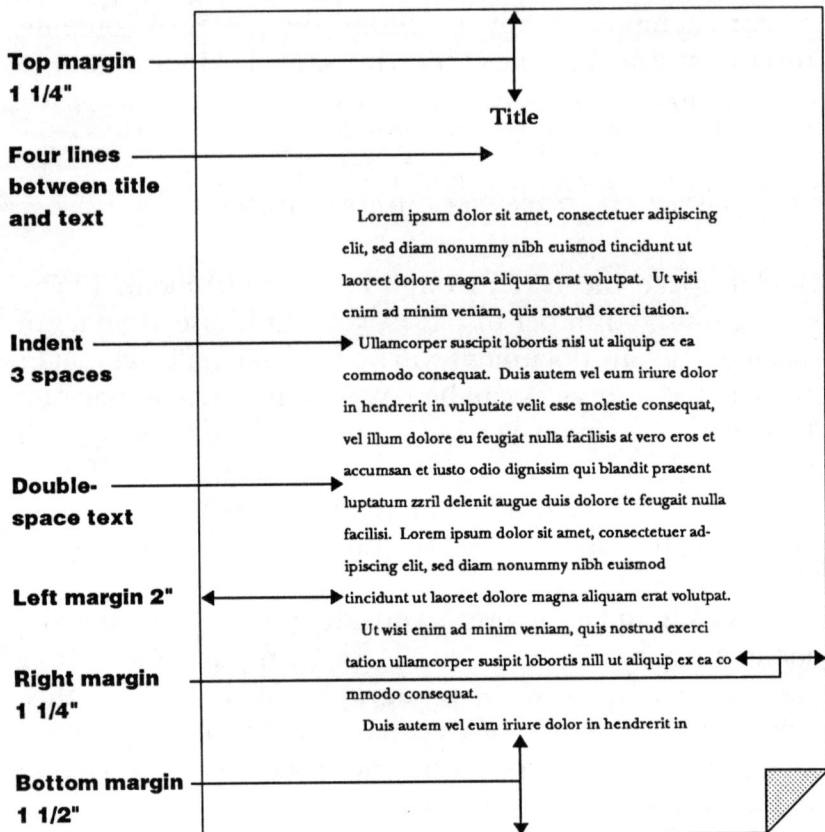

**Figure 3.10.**  A Guide to Page Layout.

The extra space allowed for the left margin (*gutter margin*) leaves room for binding. If document pages will be printed on both sides, the gutter margin must be on the inside of each page. Figure 3.11 illustrates the gutter margin.

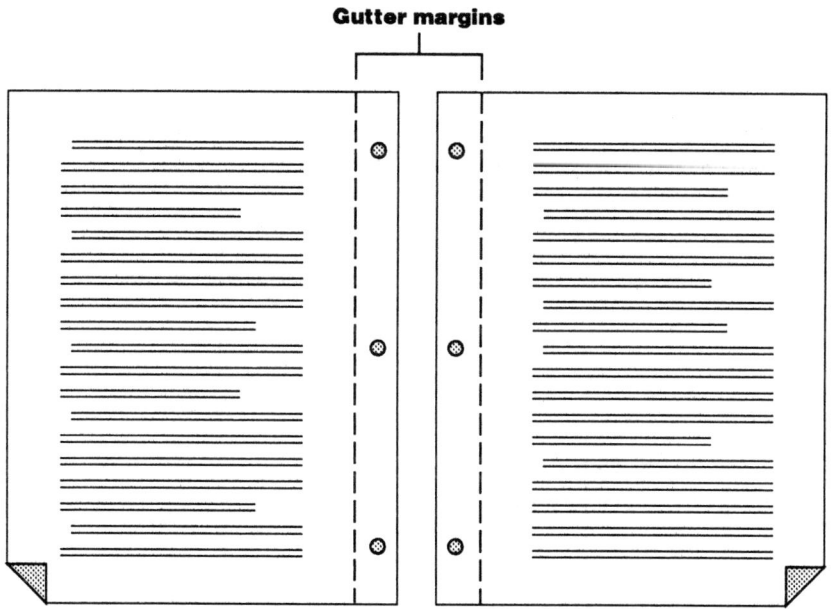

**Figure 3.11.** Gutter Margins.

## HEADINGS

Headings help your readers find their way around in the document. Ordinarily, two to four levels of headings are sufficient. And readers should be able to distinguish heading levels at a glance.

If you are using a typewriter or a word processor with limited capabilities for your final copy, you can use any one of the following, or any combination, to *format* (graphically present) your headings:

ALL CAPITAL LETTERS

**Boldface type**

<u>Underlines</u>

*Italics*

You must also decide on the linespacing to use before and after headings. Figure 3.12 illustrates typical formats and spacing for headings of various levels.

If you are using desktop publishing equipment to produce your final copy, you can choose these additional options:

○ Type sizes that reflect the heading hierarchy.

○ *Fonts* (typefaces) that differ from the font used for the text.

○ Placement of headings (for instance, placing all headings in a narrow left column and the text in a broad right column).

## ILLUSTRATIONS

When you plan a page layout, you also have to decide how to position and present illustrations.

POSITIONING ILLUSTRATIONS.   There's only one guideline for positioning an illustration: *Put the illustration as close to the accompanying text as possible, preferably immediately after it.*

How you position illustrations on your pages depends on how you will produce your final copy. For final copy—that is, typed or word-processed—you may simply interleaf the pages containing illustrations among the text pages. Or you may produce the text, leaving space for the illustrations on the pages, paste the illustrations in place, and then photocopy these pages. If you are using desktop publishing, you can simply lay out your pages, combining text and illustrations on the computer screen.

2

Lorem ipsum dolor sit amet, consectetuer adipisci g elit, sed diam
nonum nibh euismod tincidunt ut laoreet dolore magna aliquam erat
volutpat. Ut wisi enim ad minim veniam, quis nostrud.

**FIRST LEVEL HEADING**

Lorem ipsum dolor sit amet, consectetuer adipisci g elit, sed diam
nonum nibh euismod tincidunt ut laoreet dolore magna aliquam erat
volutpat. Ut wisi enim ad minim veniam, quis nostrud exerci tation.
Duis autem vel eum iriure dolor in hendrerit in vulputate velit esse
molestie consequat, vel illum dolore.

**Second Level Heading**

Lorem ipsum dolor sit amet, consectetuer adipisci g elit, sed diam
nonum nibh euismod tincidunt ut laoreet dolore magna aliquam erat
volutpat. Ut wisi enim ad minim veniam, quis nostrud.

**Third Level Heading.** Lorem ipsum dolor sit amet, consectetuer
adipiscing elit, sed diam nonummy nibh euismod tinctidunt ut laoreet
dolore magna aliquam erat volutpat. Ut wisi enim ad minim veniam,
qujis nostrud exerci tation ullamcorper suscipit.
Lorem ipsum dolor sit amet, consectetuer adipisci g elit, sed diam
nonum nibh euismod tincidunt ut laoreet dolore magna aliquam erat
volutpat. Ut wisi enim ad minim veniam, quis nostrud.

**Figure 3.12.** Headings.

PRESENTING ILLUSTRATIONS.   You can position the number, title (sometimes called a *caption*), and *legend* (explanation) either directly above or below the illustration. Figure 3.13 illustrates the most common way. Note that the number, title, and legend are positioned directly beneath the illustration and are aligned with the left edge of the illustration. Occasionally, you'll see them centered.

Illustrations, such as diagrams or photographs, sometimes include *callouts* (brief explanations of the various parts of the illustration). Tie the callout to the part it explains with a line (leader) or an arrow. Figure 3.14 shows a diagram with callouts.

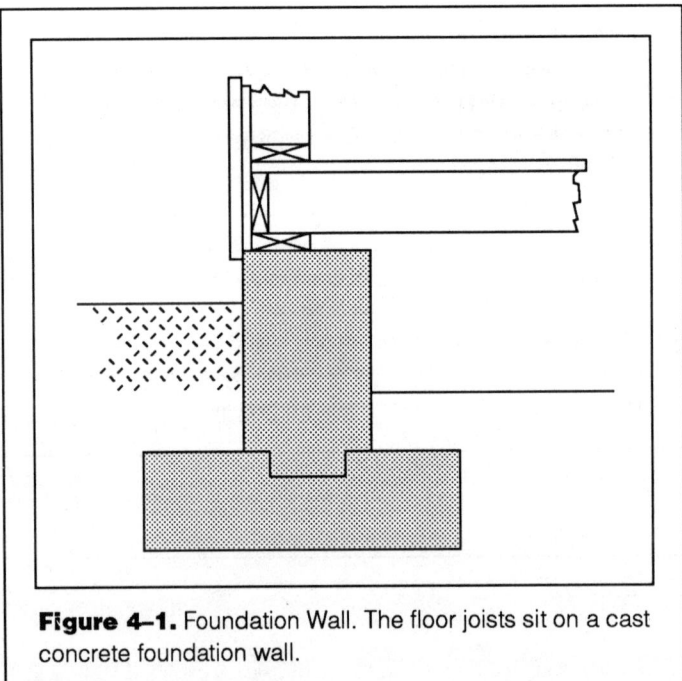

**Figure 4–1.** Foundation Wall. The floor joists sit on a cast concrete foundation wall.

**Figure 3.13.**  Number, Title, and Legend for an Illustration.

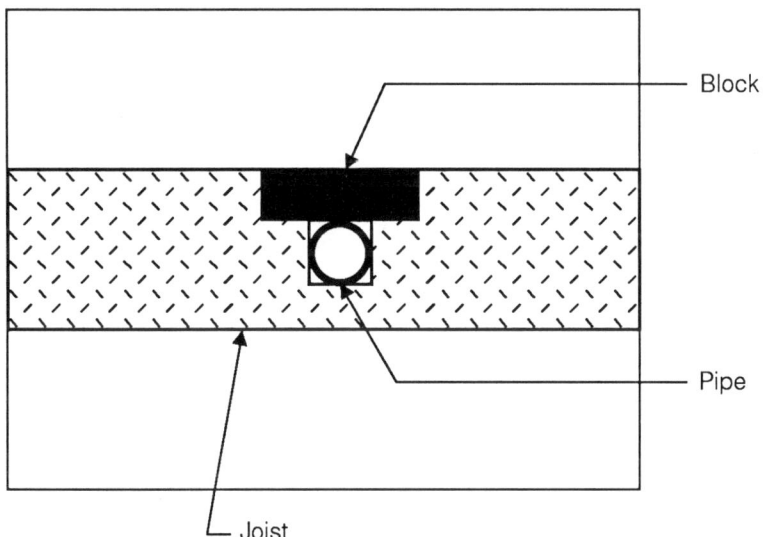

**Figure 3.14.** Illustration with Callouts.

In cases where callouts are numerous or interfere with the illustration's graphics, itemizing the elements and listing the callouts beside the illustration will make them easier to read. Figure 3.15 illustrates this method.

If you don't have the services of a graphics department or a printer, presenting your illustrations in a consistent and attractive way can be difficult. Here are some guidelines that can help:

○ Keep your illustrations within the text area of the page. Don't let them intrude into the margins.

○ Put a standard border around each illustration to make their appearance similar and their size consistent. The borders might all be the same width (usually the width of the text area) but have heights that vary.

○ Reduce or enlarge illustrations as necessary to fit within the border.

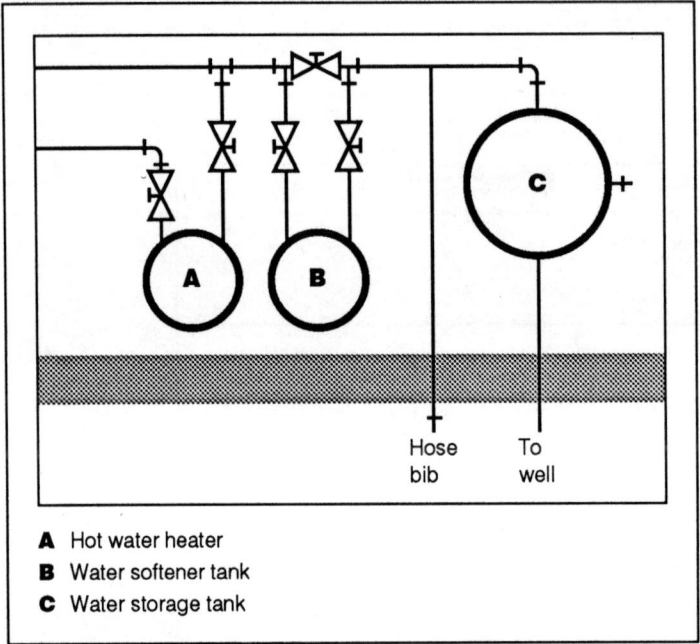

**Figure 3.15.**  Illustration with Enumerated Callouts.


The before-and-after example in Figure 3.16 shows how borders improve the appearance of illustrations. In the "after" example, one illustration was enlarged on a photocopy machine to better fit within the border.


SPECIAL TEXT

Some text needs special treatment. You may need to emphasize words or phrases or set apart longer parts of the text.

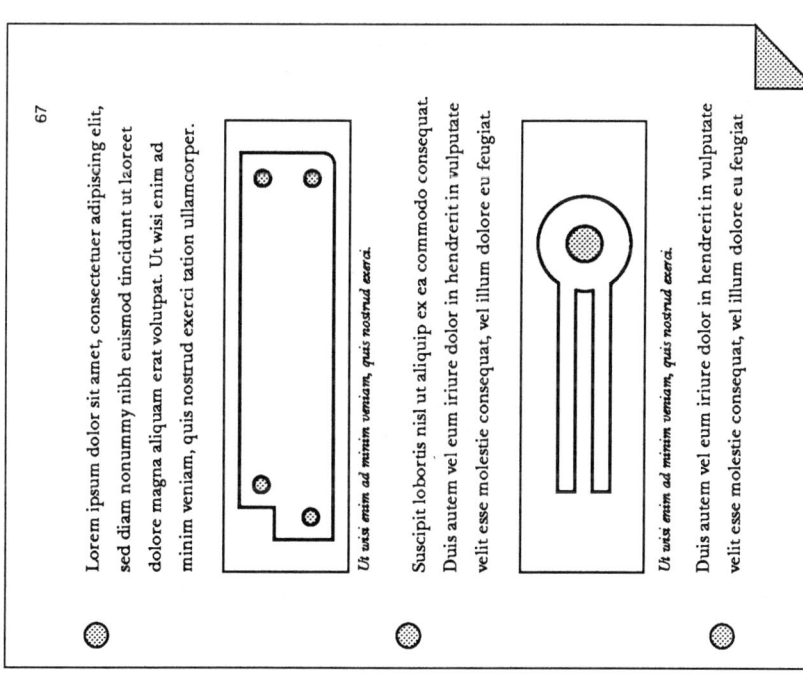

**Figure 3.16.** Putting Borders Around Illustrations.

When you want to emphasize certain words to draw them to the readers' attention, you can use:

*Italics*

**Boldface type**

<u>Underlines</u>

You may have various categories of words that need different types of emphasis. For example, in most documents, terms new to the reader are italicized, and warnings are in bold type or in full capital letters. Decide on one kind of emphasis for each of your categories.

When you have several categories of terms, each with a different type of special emphasis, you should include an explanation at the beginning of the document. Here is an example from a computer manual:

CONVENTIONS USED IN THIS BOOK

○ Commands are in all capital letters.
　Choose LIST.

○ Keys that you are to press are enclosed in parentheses.
　Press (Alpha Lock).

○ Variables or text that you are to enter are indicated with italics.
　COPY *filename* (Return).
　Type *EXEC E.GAF.MPRO* (Return).

Your document may also contain segments of text, such as quotations, examples, or displays, that you want to set off from the main text.

Lengthy quotations or quotations that you wish to emphasize should be single spaced and indented from the main text on the left as in this example.

L. G. Leonard's opening remark drew an appreciative chuckle

from the crowd.

> Computerization is not the solution to all of our problems.
> It is, however, a beginning.

Leonard was referring to the recent purchase of a new

computer system. . . .

You can also indent examples and displays to set them off.

An example of clock specification is

    XYZ.C4-6 L

which states that the clock signal goes from high to low at time 6.

Here is another example of a display. Note that it is double spaced like the main part of the text for reader convenience.

We know how to eliminate the multiplicative notation by

expanding the clause $n = h \times k$ to read

> a class of $n$ members falls into $h$ parts having
> $k$ members each.

If you can print in more than one typeface, you might also choose to show examples and displays in a typeface that contrasts with the one used for the main text. Examples of computer displays, for instance, are often set in a typeface that is much plainer and simpler than the one used for the main text.

Computer displays should duplicate as closely as possible what readers see on the screen, especially in procedures. When you are directing the reader to enter information from the keyboard, every symbol, every space, must be exact. Here's an example:

Type the chart title after the prompt as follows:
**ENTER CHART**
**TITLE: "WESTERN U.S." <ENTER>**

## LISTS AND PROCEDURES

Readers find lists and procedures easier to follow when you use a consistent format. Decide the answers to these questions:

○ How will you indent your lists and procedures?

○ How much space will you use between the introduction and the first item in the list or the first step in the procedure?

○ How much space will you use between the list items or between the steps in the procedure?

○ Will you use bullets, asterisks, or dashes for the list items?

Here's a common way to format lists:

We need to include:
    ○ A cover.  It can be made of
      — Rubber
      — Plastic
      — Hardwood
    ○ A safety latch.

The following example shows a common way to format a procedure.

> The back-up procedures are as follows:
>
>   1. Copy all new programs.
>      a. Copy the program to a second disk.
>      b. Verify the copy operation.
>   2. Copy all newly created files.
>      a. Copy the file onto a second disk.
>      b. Verify the copy operation.
>   3. Store back-up copies at a separate location.
>   4. Maintain a file of the listings of all source programs.

## RUNNING HEADS AND RUNNING FEET

You may need running heads and running feet (sometimes called *headers* and *footers*) in your document.

Running heads appear within the top margin at a specified distance between the text and the top edge of the paper.

Running feet appear within the bottom margin at a specified distance from the bottom edge of the paper. Figure 3.17 shows the placement of both running heads and feet.

Running heads and feet do not appear on title pages or in the front matter.

## FOOTNOTES

Some documents require footnotes. Each footnote has a reference number in the text. This number is usually formatted with smaller type and with *superscript* (text positioned a little above the normal text).

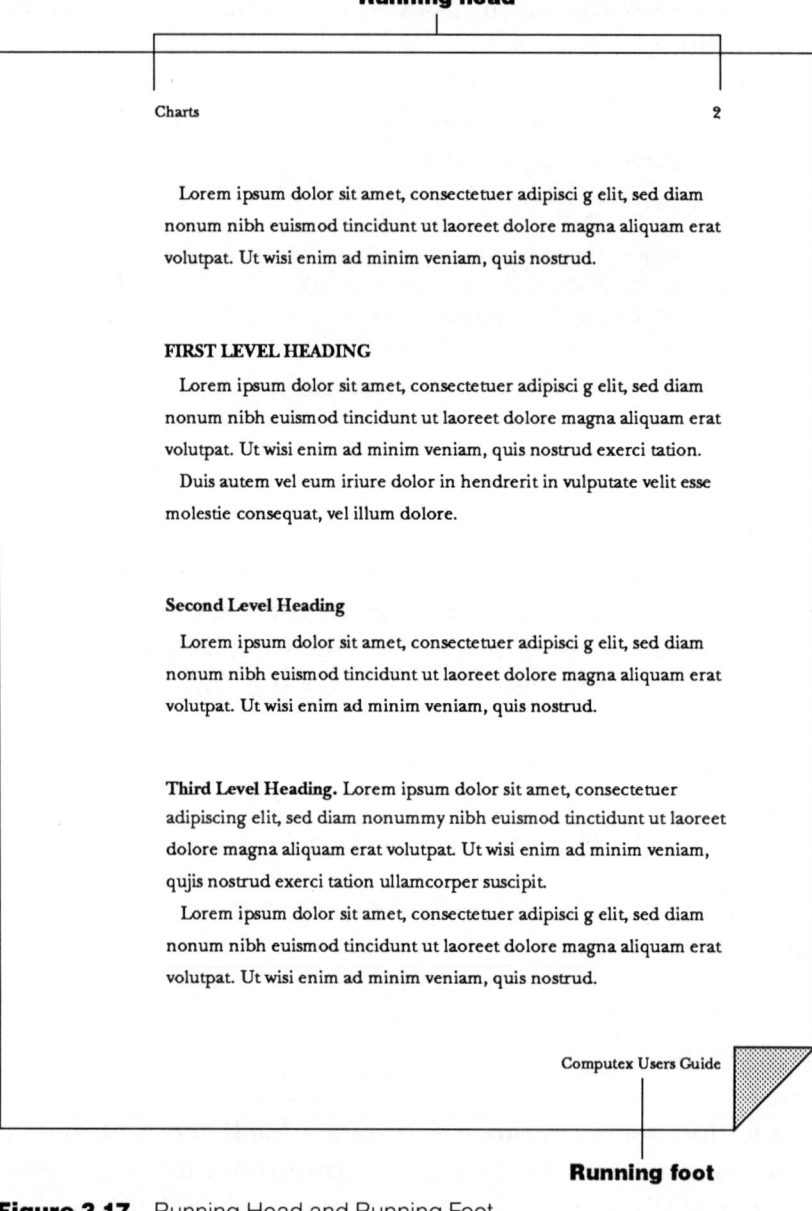

**Figure 3.17.** Running Head and Running Foot.

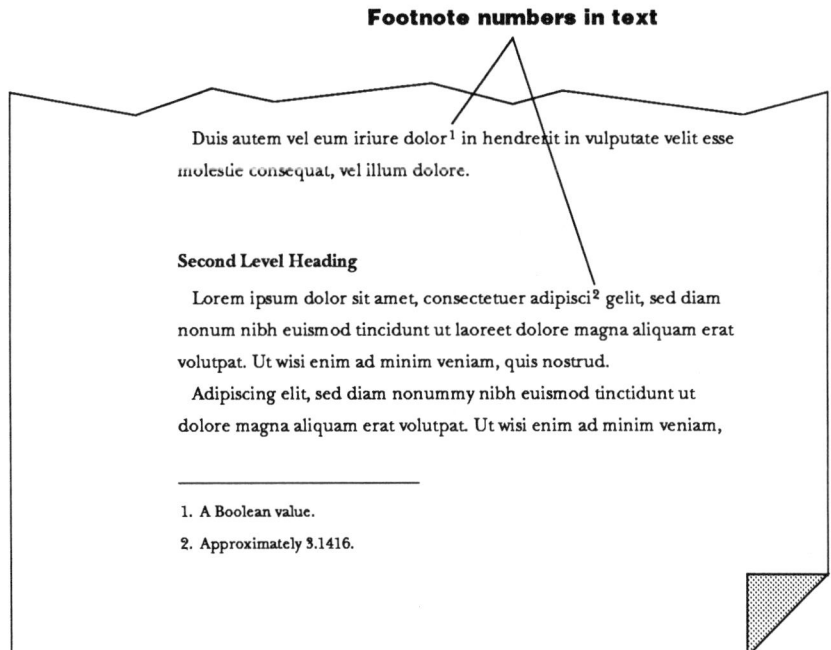

**Figure 3.18.** Footnotes.

In many documents, the footnote is given at the bottom of the page, with the reference number repeated before the footnote text, as shown in Figure 3.18.

For some documents, you may decide to have endnotes instead of footnotes. Endnotes are listed at the end of each chapter or section, or at the end of the document itself.

Footnotes for tables and illustrations are marked with symbols, such as an asterisk or star (*), dagger (†), or number sign (#). The footnotes appear below the body of the table or the illustration, not at the end of the page.

## BINDINGS

When you choose a binding for your document, you must consider:

- The size of your document
- Availability
- Cost
- Durability
- Ease of use

Some common document binders are:

- Pocket folders
- Plastic-slide folders
- Folders with brads
- Two- or three-ring notebooks

When you have the resources, you can also consider more sophisticated bindings, such as spiral or wire-o binders, or perfect binding in which pages are glued into a soft or hard cover.

Choose the most attractive binding and the one easiest for your reader to use that you can afford.

Illustrations and design are important to your document. Plan carefully and early; you and your readers will be glad you did.

You can find more examples of how to use illustrations to support your text in Chapter 12, "Writing Instructions and Persuasive Passages," and Chapter 13, "Defining, Describing, and Explaining."

# CHAPTER 4

# Ensuring Consistency in Language

CREATING A STYLE GUIDE

SAMPLE STYLE GUIDE

—Have you settled on the terms you will use for each object, process, or concept in your document?

—Have you determined the correct spelling for potentially troublesome words?

—How will you handle abbreviations and acronyms in your text?

—How are you going to punctuate series, lists, procedures, and titles for illustrations?

—Have you selected standard reference works such as a style manual, a dictionary, and a guide to English to help you maintain consistency?

—Have you collected all of the above information into a style guide?

Is "the Return key" the same as "the Enter key"? Are "the supervisor" and "the manager" the same person? Is there some reason why "free-fall" is hyphenated in some places and not in others?

Technical documents shouldn't read like mysteries with secrets that will be revealed later in the story. When we present a technical document's complex information consistently and reasonably free of error, we take a giant step forward in making it clear for our readers. Inconsistencies and small errors confuse readers, distract them from the information in the document, and plant doubts in their minds about the authority of the writer.

To maintain consistency, you need to set guidelines for *style* (the way you present written material) before you begin to write. Use a number of resources to set these guidelines, including:

O   A style guide that you create and use for a specific document.

O   A style guide created by your company that sets standards for every document it produces. Company guides are usually more comprehensive than a style guide for a specific document.

O   Style manuals used in particular fields or for government work. For instance, psychologists have a style manual, *Publication Manual of the American Psychological Association*. The United States government publishes a massive style guide, *The Government Printing Office Style Manual*, for government writing.

O   Style manuals that are comprehensive, widely used reference books. Many organizations use *The Chicago Manual of Style* as their standard reference; others use *Words into Type*.

In addition, many companies use one of the standard dictionaries and a guide to the English language. If your organization hasn't selected standard references for documentation purposes, you should obtain your own, including one of the style manuals, a good dictionary, and a guide to English. "Recommended Reference Books" at the end of this book lists selected references for each category.

## CREATING A STYLE GUIDE

Start a style guide for your document before you begin to write. Whenever you run into a troublesome word or a question about usage, you can look it up in one of your reference books or set a guideline, then add the information to your style guide. Even when your project is small, an informal style guide will be of great help to you. And when the project is complex, or when you're working with others, you and other team members, such as editors and proofreaders, will find a comprehensive style guide invaluable.

A style guide contains guidelines for usage, including:

> *Terminology:*  Should you call it the *double-bake procedure* or *Smith's procedure?*

> *Spelling:*  Is it *accommodate* or *acommodate?* Is the product name *Flexwrite* or *Flex Write?* Do you write *error free technology* or *error-free technology?*

> *Abbreviations:*  How do you handle abbreviations and acronyms? Should you spell them out or shouldn't you?

> *Quotation Marks and Italics:*  Should you put quotation marks around that special term or should you italicize it?

> *Numbers and Symbols:*  Do you write *10* or *ten?* Is it $2 \times 4 = 8$ or is it $2 \times 4 = 8?$

> *Punctuation:*  Should you use a period after each list item or not? When do you use colons?

If your organization already has an official style guide, you may only need to add guidelines for the terms, symbols, and usages that will occur in your specific document. (A sample style guide created for a specific document is given at the end of this chapter.)

Many writers also like to include a summary of the general rules for spelling, abbreviations, capitalization, and using numbers and symbols. They are then able to locate 90 percent of the information they need in a hurry, saving themselves the time and inconvenience of searching through several large texts. For your convenience, we've included such a summary in an appendix titled "Mechanics of Style" at the end of this book.

The rest of this chapter discusses the information you should include when you create a style guide.

## TERMINOLOGY

Often, when you begin to write a document on a new subject, you look through your notes and find that a certain object, process, or concept has two or three different names. For instance, if you write about a computer system, you may see the word *terminal* in one place and the word *workstation* in another, when both terms refer to the same piece of equipment. Or a process might be called by a functional name as well as by the name of its developer, as in *single-groove routing* and *Sherman's routing method.*

When readers need to know both terms, you should provide definitions. Otherwise, pick one term and use it consistently throughout your document. When you're consistent in using a term, even if it's not familiar to your readers, they are more likely to understand your meaning. You add confusion, not variety, when you use two or three terms to refer to the same thing.

## SPELLING AND SPECIAL EMPHASIS

Your style guide should show how to spell problematic words, company names, product names, and technical terms used in your document. It should also contain rules for using special emphasis, such as quotation marks and italics.

If you're using word processing software that includes a dictionary or "spell checker" feature, use it to check for spelling errors before you send your document out for review and again when you are ready to produce final copy.

COMPANY AND PRODUCT NAMES.    Company style guides may not include the organizations or products you mention in your document. Find out the official spelling of company and product names before you begin to write. Be specific; copy the capitalization, the abbreviations, the spacing, and the punctuation exactly. It may seem obvious to you, but your readers can't be sure that Bizitime Forms, Inc. is the same as BusyTime Forms Co. And don't write *the Superior Buzz Saw Company* when their letterhead says *The Superior Buzz Saw Co.* When you misspell the name of an organization or its product, you not only risk confusing your readers, you risk offending the organization as well.

Remember also that there are copyright laws. You may have to use a copyright symbol with a company name or use a registered trademark symbol with a product name the first time you mention either of them in your document. Your supervisor or your organization's legal department should be able to give you guidelines.

PROBLEM WORDS.    Certain words consistently give writers trouble. Such words as *accommodate* and *unnecessary* appear frequently in lists of misspelled words. Look up the correct spelling of any potentially troublesome words and add them to your style guide.

Some words specific to your field or your subject may be problem words. For instance, the singular of the word *strata*, which happens to be *stratum*, may repeatedly cause problems for you, your editor, or your proofreader. Add such words to the style guide once you look them up.

For some words, you have your choice of spellings. You need to decide which one you will use throughout your document. For instance, you could use either *indexes* or *indices* as the plural for the word *index*.

## ACRONYMS AND ABBREVIATIONS

Your readers may not know what a particular *acronym* (a word formed from the initial letters of a compound term, as in FBI for the Federal Bureau of Investigation) stands for, so you must spell out any acronyms the first time you mention them. If your document is long, however, you may need to spell out acronyms more than once. For instance, you might want to spell out an acronym the first time you use it in each chapter or large division of your document.

Here's an example of how to handle an acronym on its first and subsequent mentions.

*First Mention of an Acronym*

Notify the Boeing Military Airplane Company (BMAC) when your department completes the beta test.

*Subsequent Mention of an Acronym*

Testing is the responsibility of BMAC.

You should also spell out abbreviations the first time you use them or, in a longer document, the first time you use them in each major division. This example shows how to handle an abbreviation on first and subsequent mentions.

*First Mention of an Abbreviation*

Energy consumption has leveled off at 73 quads (quadrillion Btu) per year.

*Subsequent Mention of an Abbreviation*

They claimed to be consuming only 57 quads per year.

If your document uses acronyms and abbreviations extensively, provide a list of them in the front matter.

## NUMBERS AND SYMBOLS

Your document may make extensive use of numbers and symbols, perhaps setting out mathematical equations or scientific notation.

In most technical documents, quantities such as distance, length, area, volume, and so on are given in numerals (2), whereas in ordinary text they are spelled out (two).

In your style guide, include the rules you want to use in your document, clarifying them with examples. For instance, your style guide might include the following:

*Numbers*

| | |
|---|---|
| 3 cubic feet | $3'' \times 5''$ |
| 6 meters | 12 V |
| 10°30′ | the ratio 0.75 |
| 23% | |

You should also spell out rules for using special emphasis in displays of numbers and symbols. For instance, variables in an equation may be italicized or given other special emphasis. (We discuss special emphasis in Chapter 3, "Planning Illustrations and Document Design.")

## PUNCTUATION

Do you put a comma before *and*, after the next to the last item in a series? When you're introducing a list, should you use a colon? Should you put periods after each list item? How do you punctuate titles and captions for tables and illustrations? Include guidelines for punctuation in your style guide.

COMMAS IN A SERIES.   The current wisdom on punctuating items in a series is to insert a comma before the word *and*, after the next to the last item in the series.

> The operator at the scaling station should understand stick and weight scaling, statistics, and accounting.

LISTS.   Let good sense and readability be your guide when you punctuate lists. Generally, when the introductory statement is

- a complete sentence, end it with a period.

- a sentence, complete or incomplete, stating that more information is to follow, end it with a colon.

- an incomplete sentence that each list item then completes, end it with no punctuation. (You can choose not to capitalize the first letter of the list items in this case.)

Here's an example of an introductory statement that ends with a period.

> You are already familiar with many of the types of impurities that can be present in the water source.

| | |
|---|---|
| Iron | Carbon dioxide |
| Dolomite | Marsh gas |
| Gypsum | Nitrogen |
| Epsom salts | Oxygen |
| Common salt | Acid reactives |
| Manganese | Alkaline reactives |

The following example shows an introductory statement that ends with a colon because it states that more information is to follow.

Although blue is the standard color for warehouse equipment, paint the following equipment white:

- Ladders
- Handcarts
- Carryalls

Here's an example of an introductory statement that ends with no punctuation.

Excessive segregation in the material may occur because

- the discharge gate is too high above the truck body.
- the truck body is too large for the load.
- the discharge gate opens improperly.

You also need guidelines for punctuating list items. Always end complete sentences with periods. Generally, you won't use periods after incomplete sentences. Some writers, however, prefer to end lengthy, incomplete sentences with periods. Whichever style you choose, be sure to keep the items in each list consistent.

The list items in the following example are complete sentences and end with periods.

Before you begin the drill, you must gather adequate information.

- Find out how many will participate.
- Make a list of necessary equipment.
- Find out what equipment is on hand.

The list items in the example below are long sentence fragments and end with periods. (The periods are optional.)

The following types of wormholes fall into a questionable category.

    ○ Pin wormholes 1/16″ in diameter and under.

    ○ Small wormholes over 1/16″ and under 1/4″ in diameter.

    ○ Large wormholes over 1/4″ in diameter.

The list items in the following are short sentence fragments and do not end with periods.

This section will cover:

    ○ Rules and regulations

    ○ Employee benefits

    ○ Lunch breaks

PUNCTUATING PROCEDURES.   Guidelines for punctuating procedures are similar to those for punctuating lists.

○ When the introductory statement is a complete sentence, end it with a period.

○ When the introductory statement is an incomplete sentence, stating that more information is to come, end it with a colon.

○ When the introductory statement is an incomplete sentence completed by each step in the procedure, end it with a colon.

○ End each step in the procedure with a period.

PUNCTUATING CAPTIONS AND LEGENDS.  Illustrations, charts, graphs, photographs, and tables in your text should have identifying numbers and *captions* (titles). Occasionally, they'll need a *legend* (explanation) as well. Here are suggested guidelines for punctuating captions and legends for illustrations.

- O  End the number with a period.
- O  End the caption with a period. (Each word, except articles or prepositions with five letters or less, begins with a capital letter.)
- O  Punctuate the legend as you would any normal sentence.

You may place the caption and legend either directly above or directly below the illustration. Here's an example:

Figure 3.5.   Basic Parts of a Water System.
Here you see a jet unit pump, a hydropneumatic storage tank, and a device for controlling air volume in the storage tank.

## SAMPLE STYLE GUIDE

The following style guide is for a brochure that summarizes well construction and pump installation. The organization sponsoring this pamphlet does not have its own official style guide, but does use one of the standard style manuals.

STYLE GUIDE

SPELLING

**AB**

annular

aquifer

atmospheric

basalt

bore-hole

**CDE**

chlorination, chlorinators

dolomite

epsom salts

**GHIJ**

gpm (gallons per minute)

gloubers salts

hydropneumatic

impellor

**KLMN**

**OPQR**

psi (pressure per square inch)

pathogenic, nonpathogenic (*not* non-pathogenic)

Portland cement

potability

**STUV**

siphonage

stratum (singular), strata (plural)

submersible

**WXYZ**

water-bearing sand

NUMBERS

Use numerals (4) for numbers in text.
   (The envelope should be 4 to 6 inches thick.)

Hyphenate numbers with measurements.
   (4-inch to 6-inch envelope)

Area measurements
   (4 ft. × 4 ft.)

PUNCTUATION

Place a comma after the next to last item in a series, before *and*.

(Consider equipment, material, and depth.)

Follow this style to punctuate lists. Keep the following objectives in mind:

- ○ Information must be accurate.
- ○ Information must be timely.
- ○ Information must be applicable.

Setting style guidelines and following them not only improves your document, it makes your work easier. You gain the reader's confidence by being consistent and careful and your attention to the little things makes your document understandable, professional, and authoritative.

# PART TWO

# OUTLINING YOUR DOCUMENT

CHAPTER 5

# Basics of Outlining

CLASSIFICATION AND PARTITION

SUBORDINATION

LOGICAL ORDER

—Do you outline your documents using the basic techniques of classification, partition, and subordination?

—Do you arrange information in a logical order?

We all learned how to organize and outline a term paper or a thesis in high school or college. In this chapter, we will briefly review the basics of classification and partition, subordination, and logical order. Other chapters in Part Two describe how to organize and outline specific types of documents. Diagrams show the modules in each type of document and how to arrange them.

## CLASSIFICATION AND PARTITION

When we group similar items together into categories, we classify them. For instance, in a report on printers for home computer users, you might classify the printers this way to arrive at a list of topics:

```
Dot matrix
Daisy wheel
Laser
```

When we divide something into its parts so that readers will have a clearer picture of it, we partition it. For instance, if you were to write a report on a water system, you might partition the document into sections like this:

> Source of water supply
> Pumping equipment
> Storage equipment
> Control devices
> Distribution system
> Water treatment equipment

You would devote a section then to each one of these topics.

## SUBORDINATION

After you decide on your main topics, whether by classifying or partitioning, decide on your subordinate topics. For instance, under the topic "Control devices" in the report on the water system, you might discuss subordinate topics like this:

> Control Devices:
> > Pressure switch
> > Thermal overload switch
> > Air volume control
> > Pressure relief valve
> > Lightning protectors
> > Low water level cut-off switch
> > Loss-of-prime switches

You would then arrange subordinate topics under each of the other major topics.

## LOGICAL ORDER

Every time we organize our material in a sequence that will make sense to readers, we use a logical order. Often, we do this unconsciously, unaware that we are using a formal technique. Knowing how to use the many logical orders can make organizing and writing documents easier. Here are descriptions of the most common logical orders.

### CHRONOLOGICAL ORDER

When we write instructions, telling our readers what to do, step by step, we arrange material in chronological order. We also use chronological order to organize procedures and to describe processes and events. For instance, if you report on how a new mail delivery system works, you might use chronological order to divide your report like this:

> Receiving Mail from the Post Office
> Sorting Mail
> Delivering Mail
> Picking Up Outgoing Mail
> Sorting and Bundling Mail
> Delivering Mail to the Post Office

### SPATIAL ORDER

To describe an unmoving object, moving from left to right or right to left, from bottom to top, front to back, or inside to outside, we arrange material in spatial order. We use spatial order to describe unmoving objects, like photographs or illustrations, machines, buildings, or plots of land.

For instance, if you were to write a report describing a facility, you would start with an overall description and then use spatial order to describe the buildings one by one.

> Building A (northwest corner)
> Building B (northeast corner)
> Building C (southeast corner)
> Building D (southwest corner)

## ORDER OF IMPORTANCE

When we give readers important facts first, we arrange material in descending order of importance. You might do this for the convenience of busy decision makers who need to glean the significant information from the first few sections of a report.

When we give readers important facts last, we arrange material in ascending order of importance. You might do this when you want to achieve a dramatic climax, as in a persuasive report, or when you want readers to stay with the minor details in anticipation of the telling point at the end.

## ORDER OF UTILITY

When we give readers information that allows them to understand what comes next, we use the order of utility. For instance, before your readers can appreciate the new departmental structure you are recommending, they must first grasp the complex interactions of that department. Your preliminary organization might look like this:

> Statement proposing new departmental structure
> Description of present structure
> Why proposed departmental structure is better

## GENERAL-TO-SPECIFIC ORDER

When we classify and partition information, we arrange it in the general-to-specific order. For instance, a zoologist would present mammals before canines and canines before wolves.

## SPECIFIC-TO-GENERAL ORDER

When we give readers many specific details and then come to a conclusion or generalization based on those details, we arrange information in the specific-to-general order. We are presenting *evidence*. For instance, a naturalist might describe the specific actions of each dominant animal in many bands of gorillas before generalizing about the qualities that made them dominant. Or in recommending a particular type of copy machine, a writer might list the many ways the machine excels before concluding that it is undoubtedly the best.

## SIMPLE-TO-COMPLEX ORDER

When we present easy-to-understand information as a foundation to help readers understand more complex information to come, we use the simple-to-complex order. Many computer software manuals use this order as shown here:

Introduction
Part I, Basics of FastWord
Part II, Creating a Memo (a tutorial)
Part III, Using FastWord
Part IV, Advanced FastWord
Part V, Technical Reference

## CAUSE-TO-EFFECT ORDER

When we identify a cause and then discuss its effects, we arrange material in the cause-to-effect order. For instance, a writer's report describing why the department must revise the configuration management procedures for the central computer system might have this preliminary organization:

> Statement that configuration management system should be revised.
>
>> Reasons Why
>>> Causes loss of data
>>>
>>> Compromises security
>>>
>>> Wastes employee time

## EFFECT-TO-CAUSE ORDER

When we identify an occurrence, usually a problem, and discuss the reasons for it, we arrange material in the effect-to-cause order. For instance, if you write a report analyzing why so many floor panels fail inspection, you might organize it this way:

> Discussion of the high percentage of floor panels failing inspection
>
> Discussion of probable causes
>> Inadequate training for personnel
>>
>> Employees don't follow established procedures
>>
>> Supervision is weak

## PROBLEM-CAUSES-SOLUTION ORDER

When we write a report on a problem, explain its causes, and then report on how it has been or will be solved, we arrange information in the problem-causes-solution order. For instance, the report on the floor panels could end with a proposed solution like this:

> Discussion of the high percentage of floor panels failing inspection
> Discussion of probable causes
>> Inadequate training for personnel
>> Employees don't follow established procedures
>> Supervision is weak
> Solutions
>> New training procedures in effect
>> Supervisors directed to follow up

## COMPARE-AND-CONTRAST ORDER

When we write an alternatives analysis that compares and contrasts two or more items according to specific criteria, we arrange material in the compare-and-contrast order. For instance, your organization is considering two types of tele-communications systems. Your preliminary outline for the report might look like this:

> System A
>> Cost
>> Efficiency
>> Training time
>> Speed
>> Service
>> Ease of installation
> System B
>> Cost, etc.

## FAMILIAR-TO-UNFAMILIAR ORDER

When we use an analogy, comparing something familiar with something unfamiliar, we arrange information in the familiar-to-unfamiliar order. For instance, you might help readers understand the level of noise a new pump will make by comparing it to the local tornado warning siren. Ordinarily, you use this order to develop paragraphs and passages, not to organize and outline. But you might begin a section of a document very effectively with a lengthy analogy.

## ACCEPTABLE-TO-UNACCEPTABLE ORDER

When we cite the clearly acceptable points of a proposal before bringing up the points readers might object to, we arrange material in the acceptable-to-unacceptable order. For instance, if you recommend the purchase of a new photocopy machine, you might discuss that it makes copies of unsurpassed sharpness and saves money because its speed saves employee time—before you discuss the extra cost per copy.

CHAPTER 6

# Outlining Reports and Memos

—What are the goals of your report or your memo?

—What are the needs of your readers?

—Can you list the main points you want to make in your document?

—Do you know what modules go into your particular type of report? Your memo?

—Are you ready to organize and outline your report or your memo using basic techniques of classification, partition, subordination, and logical order?

What makes a report different from other documents? You write reports to present and analyze information for your readers. If your report is short, informal, and prepared in-house, it may be in the form of a memo. Memos, as anyone who has ever worked in an office knows, are often abbreviated versions of almost every type of report imaginable. This chapter discusses reports first, describing the four most common types, and then covers the ubiquitous memo.

All reports, no matter what type they are, contain similar modules and share the same basic organization. Before you outline your report, you might want to review your document plan and refresh your memory about the document's goals and about the readers and their needs. Then, with this information in mind, you can decide on the points you need to make and the topics you should discuss to achieve your goals and meet the readers' needs.

## STANDARD REPORT MODULES

The main text is the substantive part of any report, and that is what we'll cover in this chapter. Figure 6.1 illustrates the standard modules in a report. (For examples of back matter and front matter modules, see the sample documents in Chapter 16.)

*THE INTRODUCTION:*

| | |
|---|---|
| *Topic definition* | State what the topic is and describe it briefly. You might include a summary of results, if appropriate. |
| *Document's goals* | Describe what you want to accomplish with the document. |
| *Intended readers* | Describe the readers for whom the document is intended. |
| *Information: sources and methods* | Describe your sources—other documents, studies, books, journal articles, conferences, experts—or your methods of obtaining the information. |
| *Limits of report* | Describe exactly what the report will and won't cover. |

| | |
|---|---|
| *Working definitions* | When you have five or fewer terms to define, add this module. For more than five, include a "Terms and Acronyms" module in the front matter. |
| *Background* | Include this module if you need to provide background information to help readers understand your discussion. |
| *Topics for discussion* | List the topics you'll discuss in the report. |

THE DISCUSSION:

| | |
|---|---|
| *Topic A, B, etc.* | Include as many topic modules as you need. In some reports, these will be evidence for and evidence against a recommended action. In other reports, the topics will be the criteria you analyze in the report. |

THE CONCLUSION:

| | |
|---|---|
| *Summary* | Summarize the points you made in the discussion. |
| *Overall interpretation* | If necessary, give readers a broad interpretation of the information in the report. |
| *Conclusion or recommendation* | Depending on your goals, end the report with either a conclusion or a recommendation. |

| Front matter | Title page | List of figures and tables |
| | Letter of transmittal | Terms and acronyms |
| | Table of contents | Abstract |

| Main text | Introduction | Topic definition |
| | | Document's goals |
| | | Intended readers |
| | | Information: sources and methods |
| | | Limits of report |
| | | Working definitions |
| | | Background |
| | | Topics for discussion |
| | Discussion | Topic A (or criteria A) (or evidence for) |
| | | Topic B, etc. (or criteria B, etc.) (or evidence against) |
| | Conclusion | Summary |
| | | Overall interpretation |
| | | Conclusion or recommendation |

| Back matter | Appendices | Index |
| | References | |

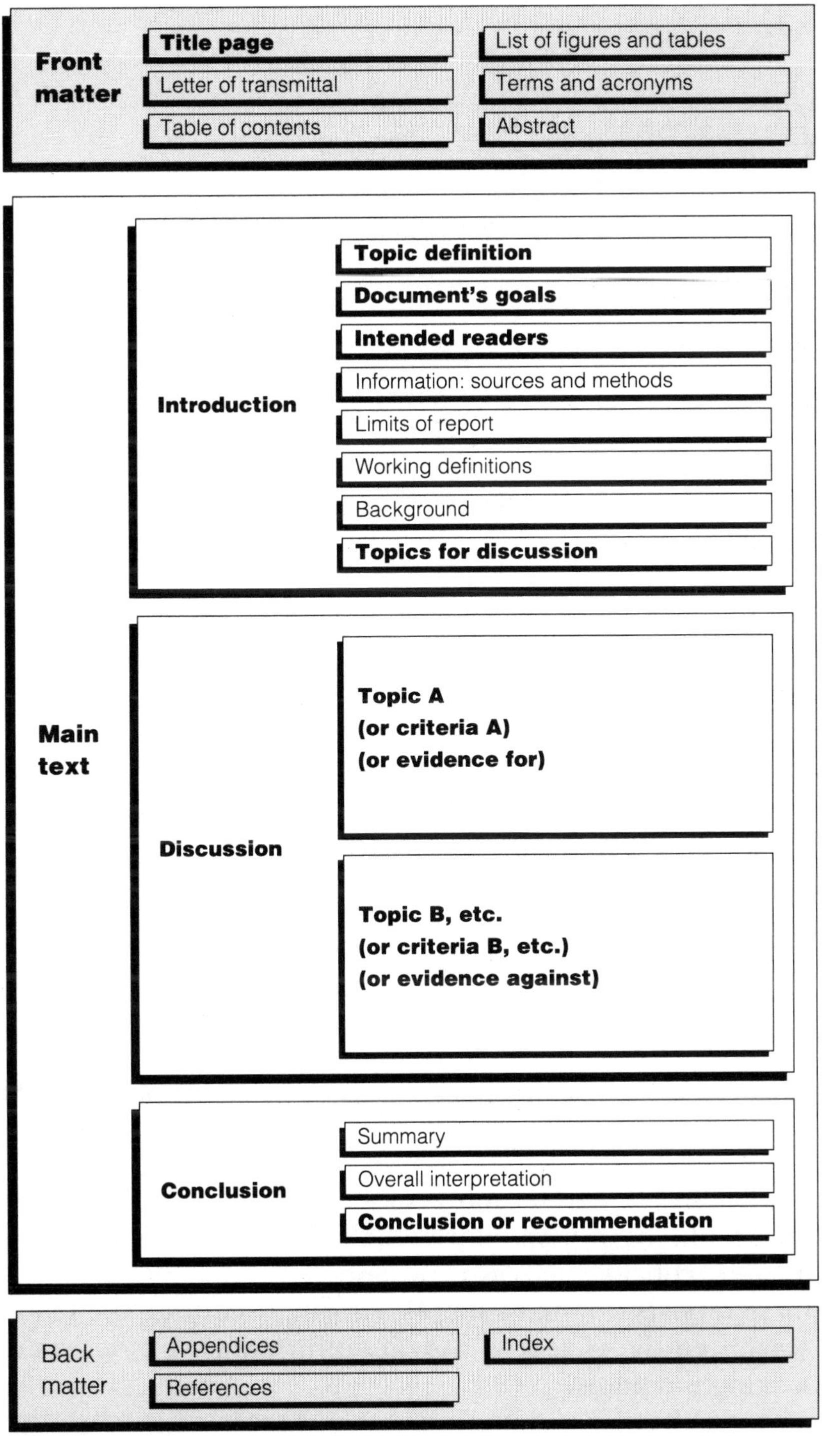

**Necessary modules**   Optional modules

**Figure 6.1.** Modules in a Report.

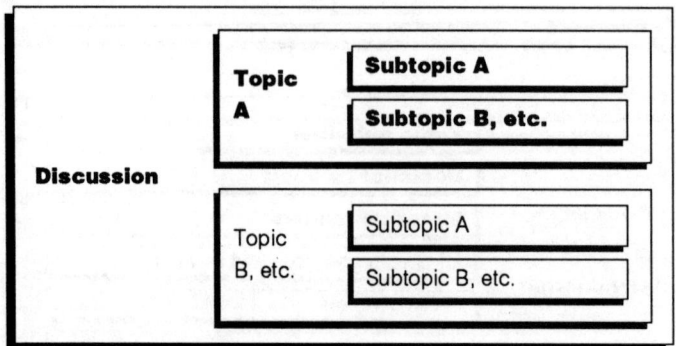

**Figure 6.2.** Subtopics in a Report.

MODULES FOR COMPLEX DISCUSSIONS.   Many times your subject will be complex; the topics in your discussion will require subtopics, as illustrated in Figure 6.2.

The way you develop a discussion varies according to the type of report you are writing, whether it is a study or research report, an alternatives analysis, a recommendation report, or a feasibility study.

## OUTLINING REPORTS

### OUTLINING STUDIES AND RESEARCH REPORTS

Studies and research reports describe, explain, and analyze the results of studies or research. They may or may not include conclusions or recommendations. The goals of these reports can be to simply inform or educate the readers. Often the goal is to provide information for decision-making purposes.

In a study or research report, the logical orders that are usually the most helpful are: simple-to-complex order, general-to-specific order, and order of utility.

OUTLINING THE DISCUSSION.    Figure 6.3 shows the modules that make up the discussion in a study or research report.

Each topic contains the following modules:

○ *Topic definition*—to announce and define the topic.

○ *Supporting information*—reports all of your findings on this particular topic.

○ *Summary or conclusion*—Sometimes you'll summarize each topic. Other times, you'll summarize all of the topics at the end of the discussion.

SAMPLE RESEARCH REPORT OUTLINE.    How can you use the information in a document plan and then apply basic outlining techniques? Let's say, for example, you're writing a report on how to verify compliance with a nuclear test ban. This is a highly technical subject for a general audience. The document plan states that the goal is to educate the readers, who are not knowledgeable in the subject matter. The document plan also states that the document has one point to make: verifying compliance with nuclear test bans is possible. You're not going to state this point in your report, however, but instead let the readers come to their own conclusion based on the evidence you provide. To accomplish these goals, you have to start with the simplest information, then give the readers increasingly complex information before getting to the heart of the report (simple-to-complex order).

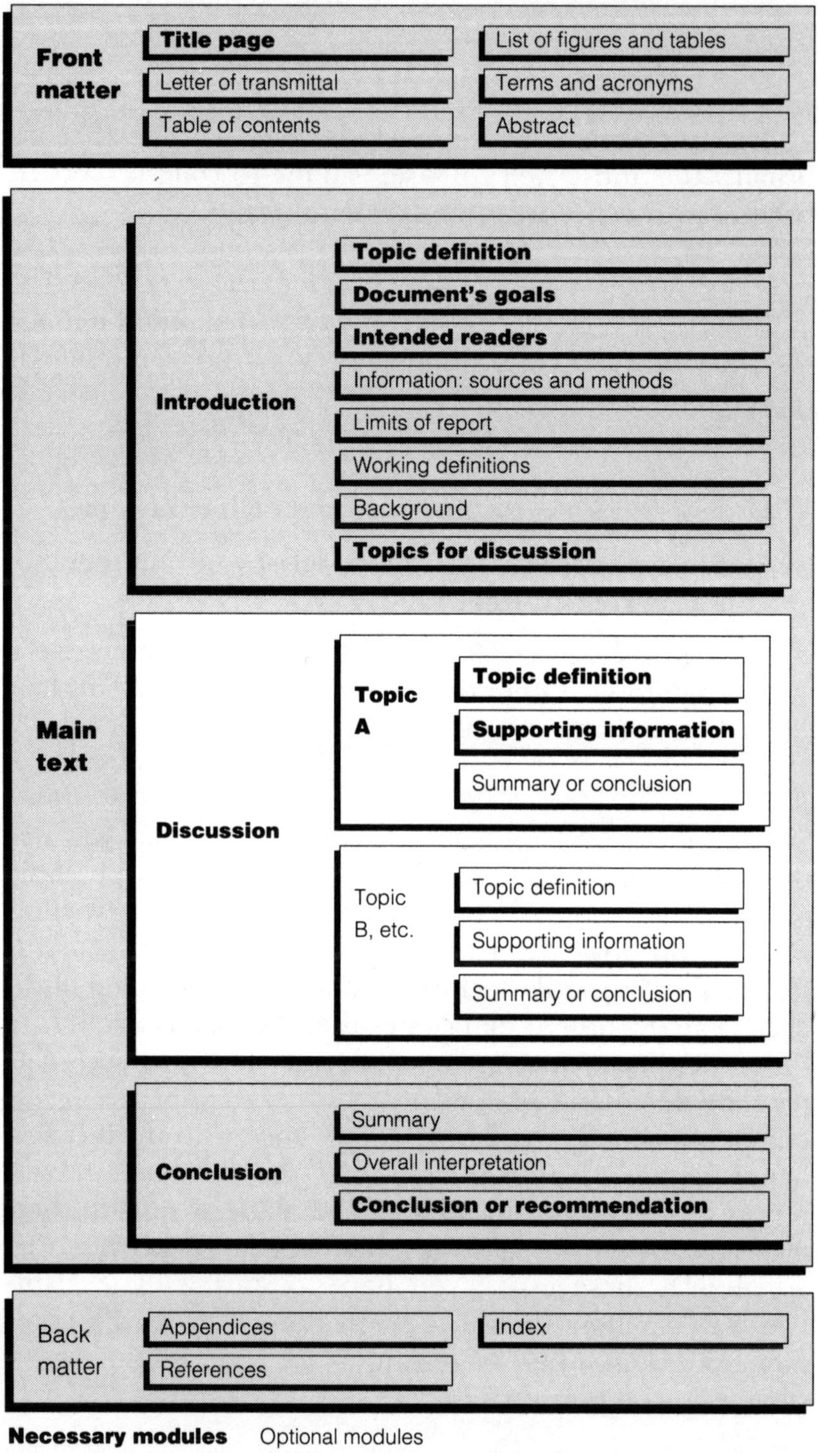

**Front matter**
- Title page
- Letter of transmittal
- Table of contents
- List of figures and tables
- Terms and acronyms
- Abstract

**Main text**

Introduction
- Topic definition
- Document's goals
- Intended readers
- Information: sources and methods
- Limits of report
- Working definitions
- Background
- Topics for discussion

Discussion

Topic A
- Topic definition
- Supporting information
- Summary or conclusion

Topic B, etc.
- Topic definition
- Supporting information
- Summary or conclusion

Conclusion
- Summary
- Overall interpretation
- Conclusion or recommendation

**Back matter**
- Appendices
- References
- Index

**Necessary modules**    Optional modules

**Figure 6.3.** Modules in a Study or Research Report.

Your preliminary list of topics for this report might read like this:

○ The four types of seismic waves.

○ How we identify seismic waves as to force, location, depth, etc.

○ How we can tell the difference between earthquakes and nuclear explosions.

○ How we can verify compliance with nuclear test bans.

You'd divide the report into sections, one for each of these topics, and then develop the subordinate information. Adding introductory material and a conclusion, your preliminary outline might look like this:

*RESEARCH REPORT OUTLINE*

    I. Introduction
       A. Statement introducing subject matter
       B. History of attempts to verify that nuclear tests have not taken place
       C. List of topics of this report
    II. Discussion
       A. The four types of seismic waves
       B. How we identify seismic waves
           1. Force
           2. Location
           3. Depth, etc.
       C. How we can tell the difference between earthquakes and nuclear explosions
           1. Force
           2. Location
           3. Depth, etc.
       D. How we can verify compliance with nuclear test bans
    III. Conclusion
       A. Summary

SAMPLE STUDY OUTLINE.   Here's an outline of the main text of a document reporting on the results of a study. The report analyzes the possible causes of frequent worker illness in a plant. The writer listed all of the effects, then analyzed the cause (effect-to-cause order). You can also see how the writer partitioned the big topic (the company plant) into sections (the individual buildings).

*STUDY OUTLINE*

   I. Introduction
      A. Topic Statement
      B. Summary of Results
      C. Reasons for Undertaking Study
         1. Frequent sickness of office workers
         2. Frequent complaints about poor ventilation
      D. Description of Buildings Studied
         1. Building 1A
            a. Size
            b. Age
            c. Ventilation system
         2. Building 1B
            a. Size
            b. Age
            c. Ventilation system
         3. Building 1C
            a. Size
            b. Age
            c. Ventilation system
      E. Methodology Used
         1. Visits of independent judges
            a. Workers present
            b. Workers not present
         2. Description of tests and measurements
            a. Carbon dioxide, indoors and outdoors
            b. Carbon monoxide, indoors and outdoors
            c. Particulate matter, indoors and outdoors
            d. Rate of air exchange traced by generating
               and tracking gas
         3. Procedure
            a. Schedule and duration of visits
            b. Order in which tests performed
            c. Outdoor conditions on visitation days
      F. Topics covered in this report.

II. Discussion of Results
    A. Building 1A
        1. Introductory statement
        2. Test results
            a. Workers present
            b. Workers not present
        3. Interpretation
    B. Building 1B
        1. Introductory statement
        2. Test results
            a. Workers present
            b. Workers not present
        3. Interpretation
    C. Building 1C
        1. Introductory statement
        2. Test results
            a. Workers present
            b. Workers not present
        3. Interpretation
    D. Comparison of indoor and outdoor measurements
        1. Statement
        2. Comparison
        3. Interpretation
III. Conclusion
    A. Summary of test results
    B. Causes of pollution
        1. Building materials
        2. Dust and fungus in ventilation system
        3. Workers smoking tobacco
        4. Chemicals used by workers
    C. Comparison with results of similar studies

## OUTLINING FEASIBILITY STUDIES

Feasibility studies are a type of report used for decision making. They help an organization decide whether it's feasible to make a change in the way they do business. For instance, a feasibility study might help them decide whether they should replace a piece of equipment, adopt a different system, change their method of production, or hire an outside contractor to do some of the work.

OUTLINING THE DISCUSSION.    Figure 6.4 illustrates the modules for a feasibility study.

| | |
|---|---|
| *Need or problem* | Describe the need or the problem. |
| *Description of possible solution* | Describe the possible solution. |
| *Benefits of proposed solution* | Describe the anticipated benefits of the proposed solution. |
| *Impact on plans or programs* | Analyze how the proposed solution would affect long-range plans or existing programs. |
| *Alternatives* | Describe the possible alternatives, including no action. |
| *Risks and disadvantages* | Analyze the economic, operational, or other risks involved. |
| *Cost* | Estimate the cost. |

The feasibility study is like a recommendation because it too presents evidence for and evidence against a proposed product, method, or service. The feasibility study, however, does not use persuasive tactics; it simply reports findings.

Your goal in a feasibility study is to give decision makers the information they need to make the best decision possible.

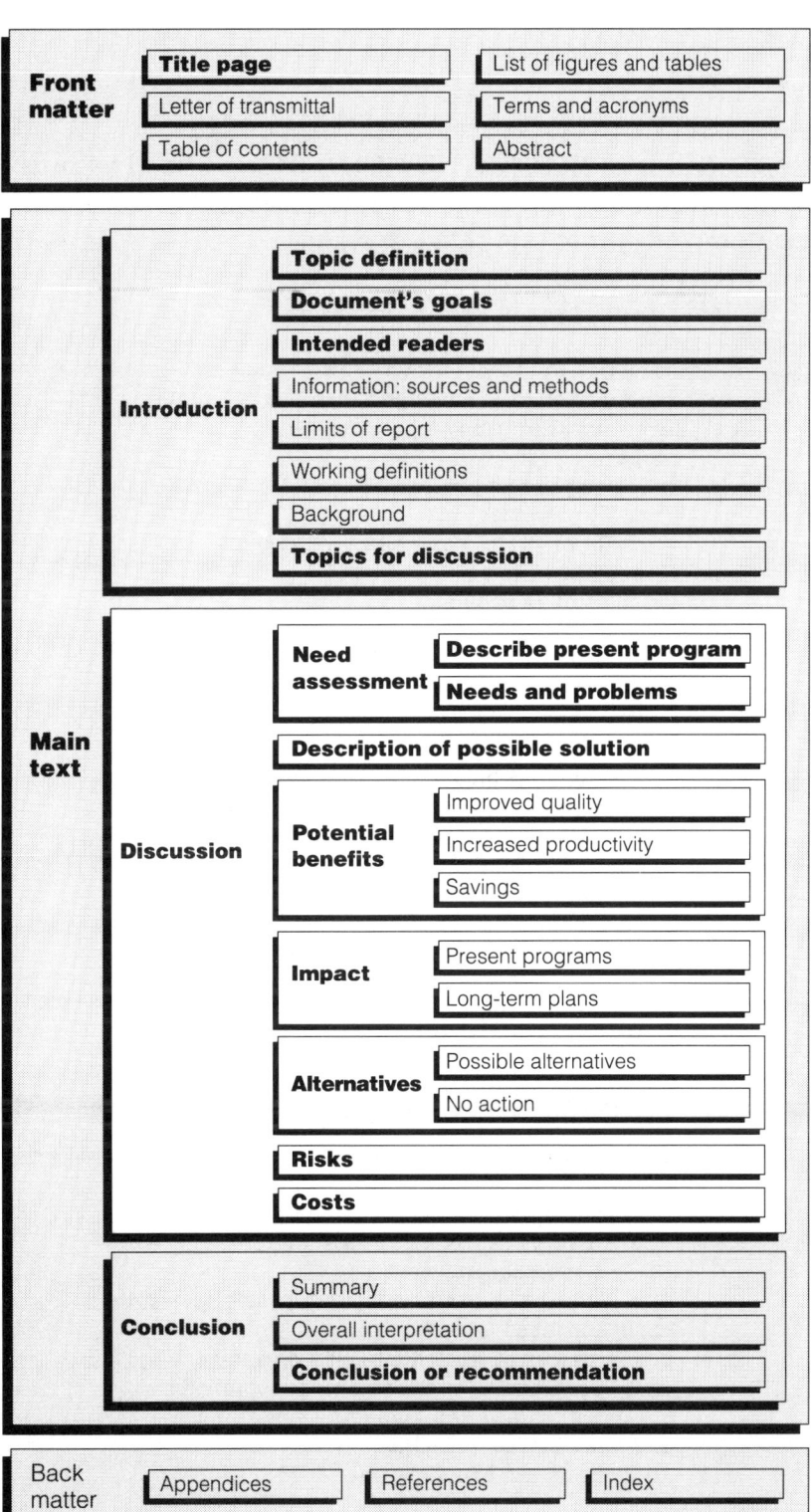

**Necessary modules**   Optional modules

**Figure 6.4.** Modules in a Feasibility Study.

SAMPLE FEASIBILITY STUDY OUTLINE.    The feasibility study outlined below analyzes the feasibility of adding an economizer unit to a pipeline system.

*FEASIBILITY STUDY OUTLINE*

I.  Introduction
    A.  Summary of goals we hope to achieve by adding an economizer unit
    B.  Scope
        1.  Description of project
            a.  Economizer unit
            b.  Description of installation process
        2.  Departments involved
    C.  Description of problem
II.  Discussion
    A.  Assessment of need
        1.  Description of present system
        2.  Problems with present system
            a.  Need better control in pumping liquids
            b.  Safety problems
            c.  High energy costs likely to get higher
    B.  Benefits of adding economizer
        1.  Improved quality
            a.  Better control in pumping liquids
            b.  Increased safety
            c.  Improvement in employee morale
        2.  Reduced energy costs
    C.  Description of impact
        1.  No impact on other operations
        2.  Reduction of costs will have a positive impact on future plans
    D.  Alternatives
        1.  No other known alternatives
        2.  Impact of no action
            a.  Continued loose control of pumping liquids
            b.  Energy costs continue at a high rate, certain to increase in future
            c.  Unsafe conditions continue, possible lawsuits
    E.  Risks and disadvantages
        1.  Disruption of work during installation
        2.  Cost of training time required for controllers
        3.  Cost of installation, including downtime
        4.  None other foreseeable
    E.  Analysis of cost of adding unit
III.  Conclusion
    A.  Discussion of benefits vs. disadvantages

OUTLINING ALTERNATIVES ANALYSES

Alternatives analyses help companies decide between two or more alternatives. In an alternatives analysis, you use a compare-and-contrast sequence to analyze the alternatives according to specified criteria. To arrange the criteria, you use the order of importance.

ORGANIZING THE DISCUSSION.   You can organize the discussion in an alternatives analysis in one of two ways. In Figure 6.5 the alternatives are the major topics. Each alternative is discussed in turn, in terms of the criteria.

Figure 6.6 shows the other way to organize an alternatives analysis, in which the criteria are the major topics.

SAMPLE ALTERNATIVES ANALYSIS OUTLINE.   As an example of an alternatives analysis, let's say that you're developing an outline for a report on competing brands of floor coverings for commercial airplanes. The report is for executives who are decision makers. The readers are knowledgeable about the field in general, but only some of them are knowledgeable about this particular subject. The goal, as in most alternatives analyses, is to give the readers enough information to make a decision. In this report, you don't have any specific points to make.

The techniques of classification, partition, and subordination are at the heart of alternatives analyses. In this report, however, assume that you've already moved beyond the classification stage because, early on, decision makers eliminated other classifications of floor carpeting in favor of synthetic blends. You can then partition the document into the top two competitors. Your subordinate topics are the criteria important to readers: fire resistance, potential for toxic gases, durability, ease of installation, appearance, and cost.

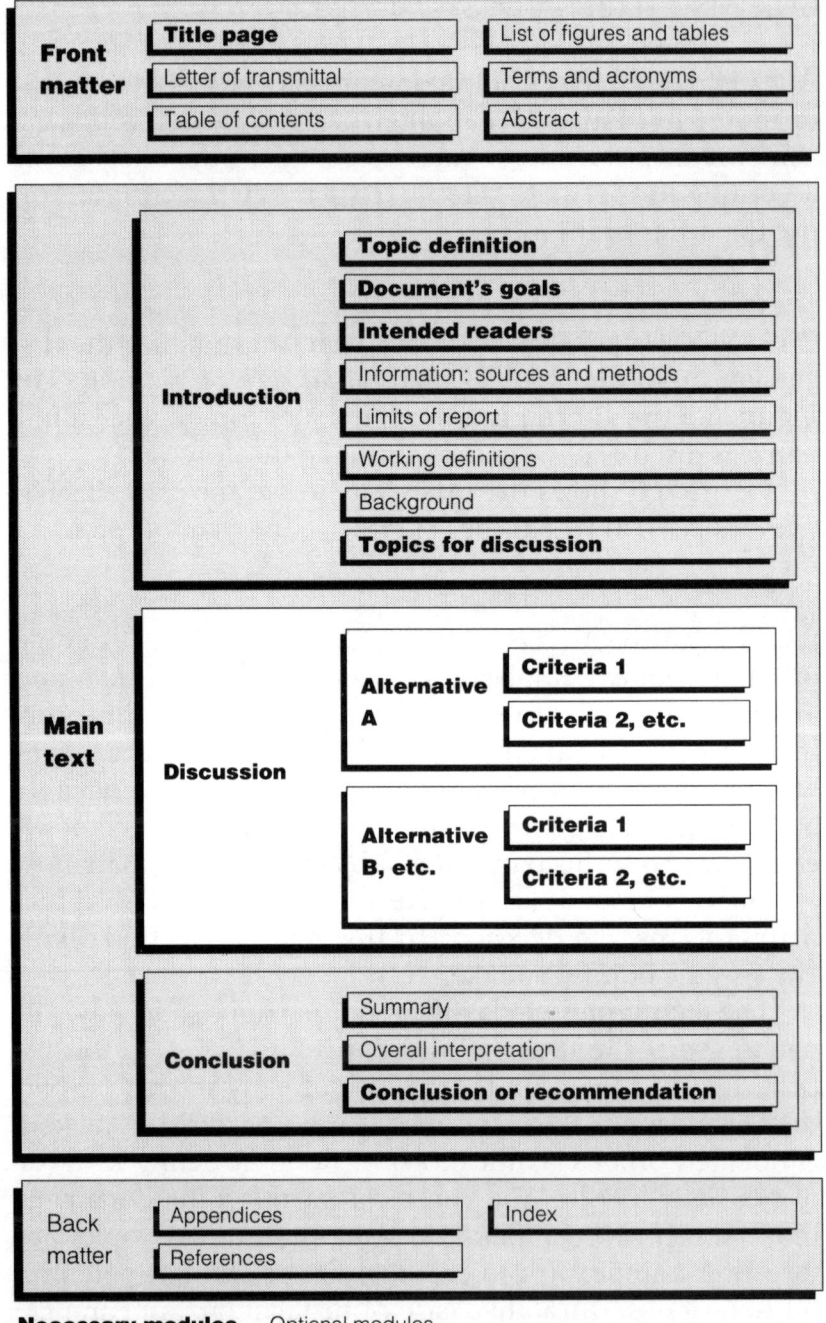

**Necessary modules**    Optional modules

**Figure 6.5.**  Modules in an Alternatives Analysis (1).

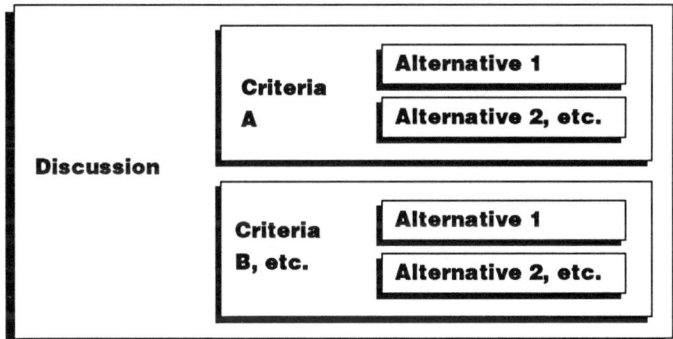

**Figure 6.6.** Modules in an Alternatives Analysis (2).

Your preliminary outline of the main text might look like this:

I. Introduction
    A. Topic statement
    B. Background explaining why synthetic blends are best
    C. Background on the two competitors
    D. Sources of information used in analysis
    E. List of floor covering manufacturers under consideration
    F. List of criteria
II. Discussion
    A. National Floor Coverings
        1. Appearance
        2. Fire resistance
        3. Potential for toxic gases
        4. Durability
        5. Ease of installation
        6. Cost
    B. United Floor Coverings
        1. Appearance
        2. Fire resistance
        3. Potential for toxic gases
        4. Durability
        5. Ease of installation
        6. Cost
III. Conclusion
    A. Summary
    B. Overall interpretation

Now, look the outline over. Have you left anything out? Since readers should also consider ease of maintenance, add that as one of the criteria. Have you arranged the criteria in the proper logical order? For the convenience of busy decision makers, it's best to arrange the criteria in order of descending importance. A table summarizing the features would be helpful to readers too. Now your outline looks like this:

*ALTERNATIVES ANALYSIS OUTLINE*

I. Introduction
   A. Topic statement
   B. Background explaining why synthetic blends are best
   C. Background on the two competitors
   D. Sources of information used in analysis
   E. List of floor covering manufacturers under consideration
   F. List of criteria
II. Discussion
   A. National Floor Coverings
      1. Durability
      2. Fire resistance
      3. Potential for toxic gases
      4. Appearance
      5. Ease of maintenance
      6. Ease of installation
      7. Cost
   B. United Floor Coverings
      1. Durability
      2. Fire resistance
      3. Potential for toxic gases
      4. Appearance
      5. Ease of maintenance
      6. Ease of installation
      7. Cost
III. Conclusion
   A. Summary
   B. Table
   C. Overall interpretation

## OUTLINING RECOMMENDATION REPORTS

Recommendation reports ask others either to take action or to support a point of view. They are similar to research reports and, sometimes, to alternatives analyses. Because the goal of a recommendation report, however, is to persuade readers, this type of report uses persuasive techniques.

Generally, you organize a recommendation with the problem-causes-solution order. You need to convince your readers that a problem or need exists, and then convince them that you can solve the problem or fill the need. To arrange the points you want to make, you can choose between the acceptable-to-unacceptable order or the order of descending importance. In some recommendations, you may also need to give readers background information (the order of utility).

OUTLINING THE DISCUSSION.    In Figure 6.7, the two major topics in the discussion are evidence for the recommended action and evidence against it. Because the acceptable-to-unacceptable order is most effective in a recommendation report, the evidence for the recommendation comes first.

*Evidence for*        Discuss each point that is favorable to the recommendation.

*Evidence against*    Discuss and refute each objection you anticipate the readers will make.

To establish a favorable attitude immediately in a recommendation report, you want to give the important evidence first (order of descending importance).

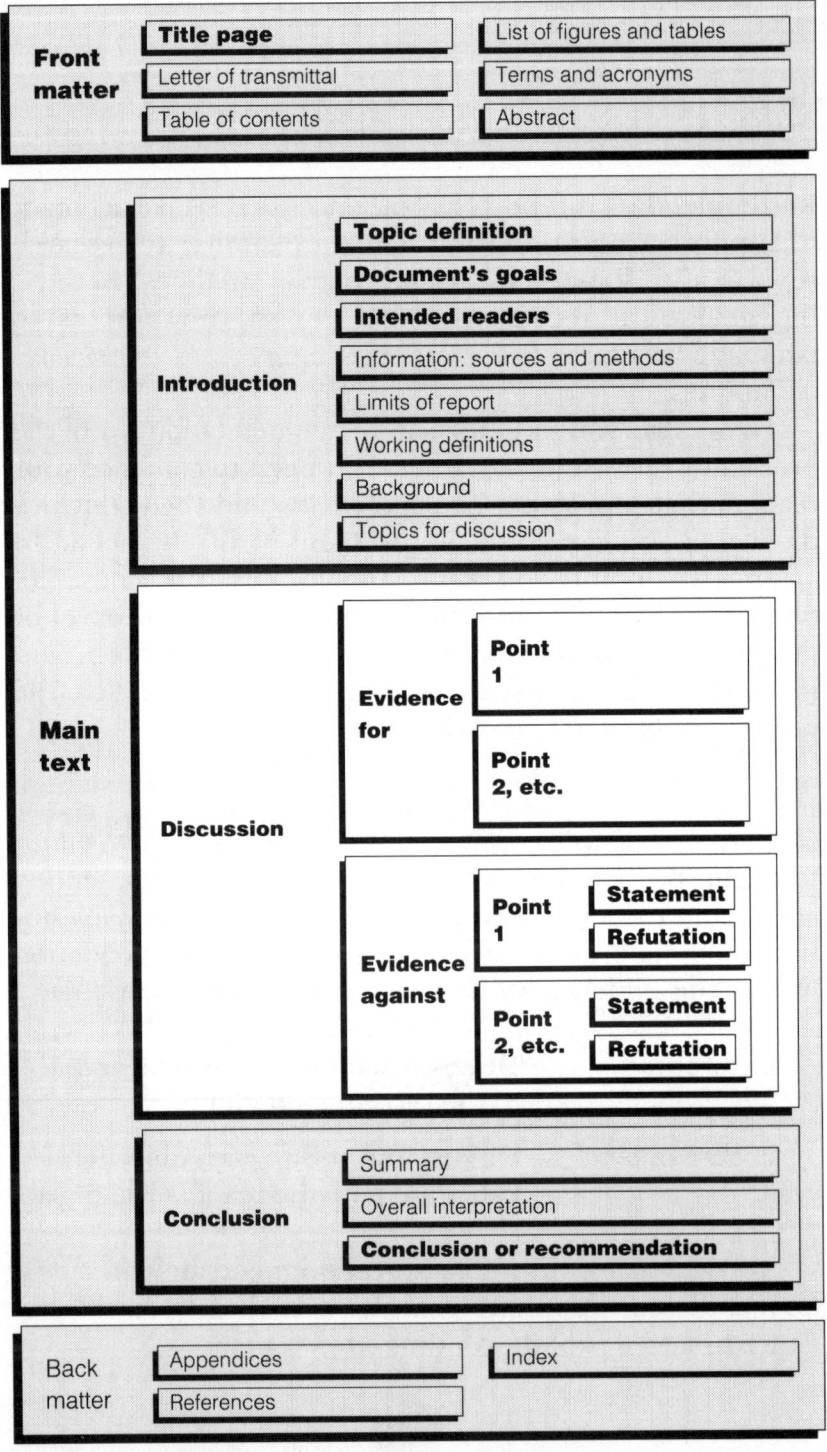

| | | |
|---|---|---|
| **Front matter** | **Title page** | List of figures and tables |
| | Letter of transmittal | Terms and acronyms |
| | Table of contents | Abstract |

**Main text**

**Introduction**
- **Topic definition**
- **Document's goals**
- **Intended readers**
- Information: sources and methods
- Limits of report
- Working definitions
- Background
- Topics for discussion

**Discussion**

**Evidence for**
- Point 1
- Point 2, etc.

**Evidence against**
- Point 1 — Statement / Refutation
- Point 2, etc. — Statement / Refutation

**Conclusion**
- Summary
- Overall interpretation
- **Conclusion or recommendation**

**Back matter**
- Appendices
- References
- Index

**Necessary modules**   Optional modules

**Figure 6.7.** Modules in a Recommendation Report.

SAMPLE RECOMMENDATION REPORT OUTLINE.   The goal of this report is to convince management that the company needs to acquire new word processing software. The writer first gives readers background information about the current process used to produce proposals (the order of utility). The writer uses the order of descending importance to arrange the evidence for and the evidence against the proposal.

*RECOMMENDATION REPORT OUTLINE*

    I. Introduction
       A. We should replace WriteMaster with WordWhiz word processing software.
       B. Our present system of producing proposals needs to be improved.
          1. Costs are too high.
          2. Proposals are late.
       C. Description of current process.
          1. Word processors use WriteMaster on microcomputer to enter text.
          2. Word processors use Mathsystem on the mainframe computer to create spreadsheets.
          3. Word processors print text and spreadsheets.
          4. Temporaries paste up pages.
          5. Secretaries make copies and distribute.
       D. Description of WordWhiz word processing program.
          1. WordWhiz creates both text and spreadsheets.
          2. WordWhiz has page-layout features that format pages before printing.
   II. Discussion
       A. WordWhiz will serve our purposes better than the current process.
       B. What WordWhiz can do for us.
          1. We can create proposals on our microcomputers, leaving mainframe free for payroll and database functions.
          2. We can cut training costs for the word processing staff because they will not have to learn how to use the mainframe.

      3. We can cut costs because we will not have to hire temporaries to do paste-up.
      4. We can improve efficiency because proposals can be created in one place under the control of one lead.
   C. Potential drawbacks.
      1. Initial cost.
         a. Initial cost would be $489 $\times$ 12 (workstations).
         b. WordWhiz will give us a 10% discount because of our volume order.
         c. We will recover our initial expenditure in nine months because of lowered costs.
      2. Word processors dislike learning new programs.
         a. Studies show people prefer WordWhiz.
         b. WordWhiz will be a plus in their job history.
      3. Efficiency will be down during training period.
         a. Studies show WordWhiz easy to learn, especially when trainees know other word processing programs.
III. Conclusion
   A. WordWhiz will improve our system of producing proposals by reducing time necessary to produce them.
   B. WordWhiz will cut our costs.
   C. The drawbacks are not serious.

## OUTLINING MEMOS

"Don't tell me the details now—send me a memo!" Memos are our all-purpose form of communication in the workplace. Typically, they contain the modules shown in Figure 6.8: the opening, the main text, and the closing.

Most organizations have a standard format for memos. (You can see the modules that most memos contain in the Chapter 16 sample.) Main text can vary greatly but every memo, even if it's very brief, should have an introduction, a discussion, and a conclusion. The example below shows the three parts of a short memo.

Introduction    The maintenance department is pleased to announce the promotion of April Allison to a new position, central coordinator.

Discussion      This position has been created to streamline maintenance and repair service within the company. April's duties will be:

  ○ Receiving requests for service from all parts of the company.
  ○ Assigning the service requests to maintenance personnel.
  ○ Following up all assignments to see that service has been performed satisfactorily.

Conclusion      We expect that the introduction of a central coordinator will improve efficiency in all divisions of the company.

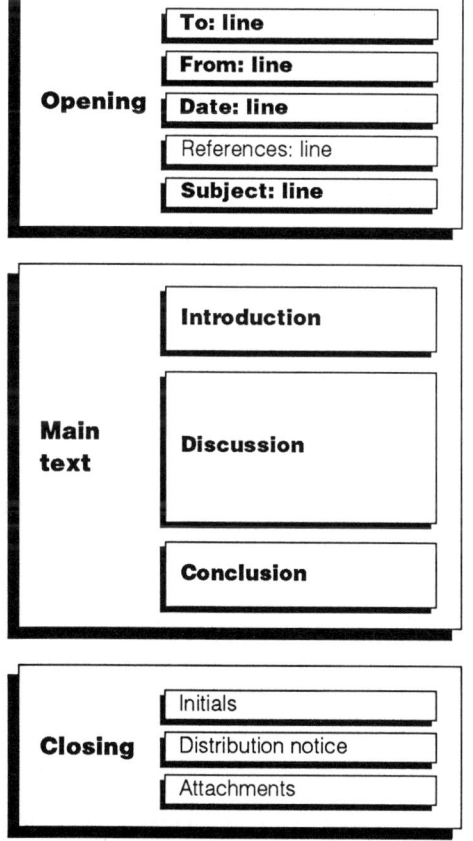

**Necessary modules**    Optional modules

**Figure 6.8.**  Modules in a Memo.

Many memos are short versions of reports, so you'll use many of the same outlining methods. For instance, a memo recommending a purchase of equipment or a change in departmental methods might be composed of an abbreviated version of the same modules used for the main text of a recommendation report, as in Figure 6.9. You may not need all of these modules, of course, and some of them will be very brief.

If you're presenting the results of a research project, you can borrow the main text modules of a research report, as in Figure 6.10. Remember to use headings in a lengthy memo just as you would in any other type of report.

## SAMPLE MEMO OUTLINE

Here's an outline for a memo, a progress report on a construction project.

> To:        All Directors
> From:      H. B. Gragg, Project Supervisor
>            Alice Foster, Construction Liaison
> Subject:   Progress Report on Plant Conversion from
>            Old LC-II Process to New 2000-SR Process
>            to Improve Coal Liquefaction Output
> Date:      May 12, 1988
>
>   I. Brief description of project
>  II. Progress on all project components
>      A. Conversion of reactors
>      B. Construction of water-treatment facility
>      C. Upgrade of solids-removal facility
> III. General conclusion
>      A. Project is one week behind schedule
>      B. We will make up time by beginning road improvements
>         ahead of schedule

The discussions, illustrations, and examples in this chapter should help you organize almost any type of report you'll ever need to write. Additionally, you can use many of the same techniques to organize your memos.

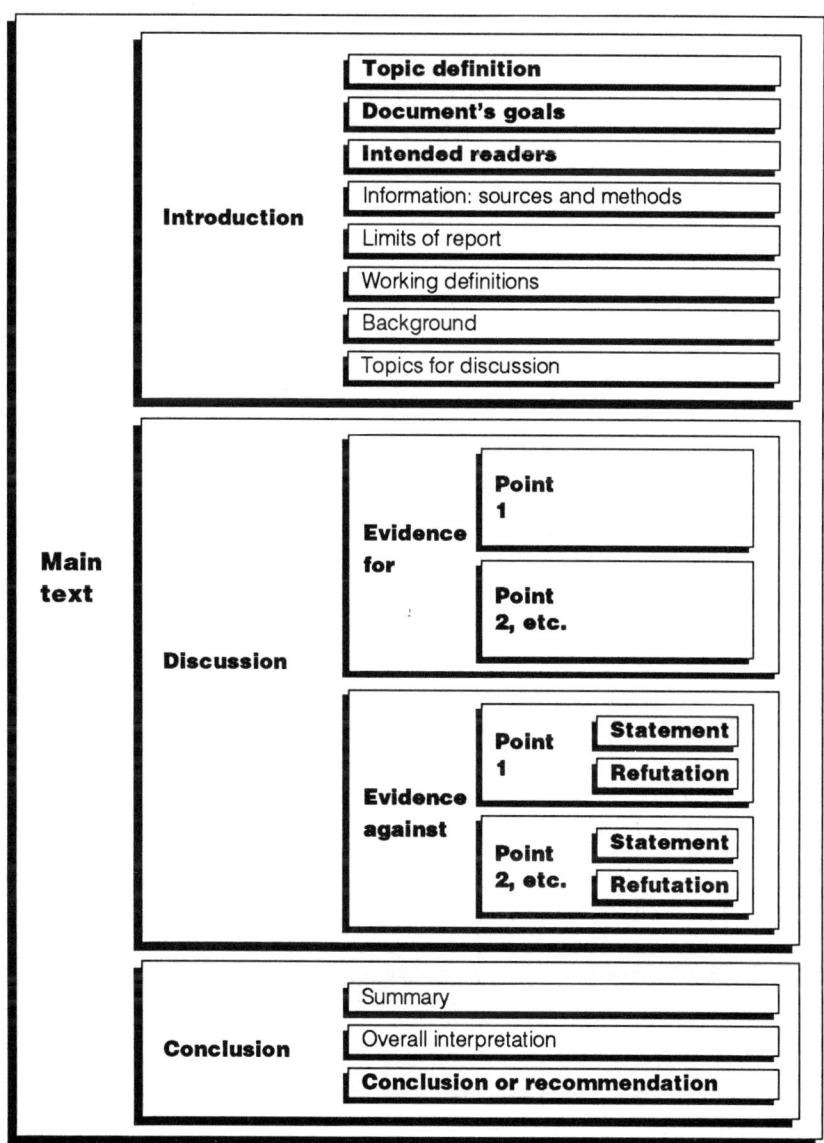

**Figure 6.9.** Modules in the Main Text of a Recommendation Report.

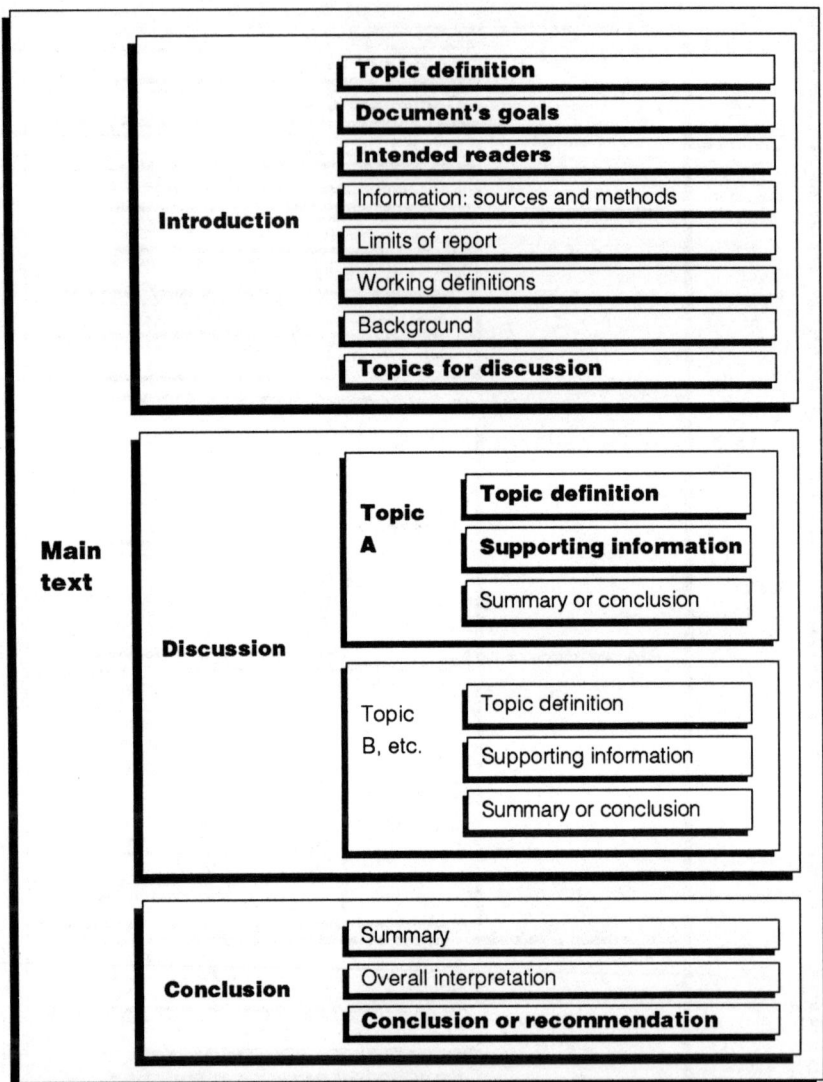

**Figure 6.10.** Modules in the Main Text of a Research Report.

# Outlining Instructional Materials

STANDARD MODULES FOR
INSTRUCTIONAL MATERIALS

CHOOSING THE RIGHT ORGANIZATION

SAMPLE OUTLINE FOR AN
INSTRUCTION BOOKLET

SAMPLE OUTLINE FOR A USER'S
GUIDE

—What are the goals of your instructional material?

—Who are your readers and what do they already know about the subject?

—What, specifically, do you want the readers to learn?

—What level of expertise do you want the readers to reach?

—Do you know which modules to include in your instructional material?

—Are you ready to organize and outline using the basic techniques of classification, partition, subordination, and logical order?

Here you go again. The new photocopy machine is jammed and, unfortunately, you were in a meeting the day the representative demonstrated how to use it. You're stuck with reading the instructions and you're praying that they're written in clear, concise English. Sound familiar? Of course it does. Today, no one can escape reading instructions, whether they are one-page directions for assembling a bookshelf or a 500-page manual explaining how to use a complicated computer system.

The method you choose to organize the instructional materials that *you* write will make a big difference to your readers. Although the organization may vary, instructional materials generally contain some standard modules. We'll look at these first. Later we'll discuss some variations to suit specific situations and goals.

## STANDARD MODULES FOR INSTRUCTIONAL MATERIALS

Most instructional materials include the modules illustrated in Figure 7.1.

The front and back matter contain the same modules you'd find in a report. (Examples of these report modules are in the sample document in Chapter 16.) The main text, while similar to that of a report, in that it contains an introduction, a discussion, and a conclusion, varies in the way you develop these modules.

*THE INTRODUCTION:*

| | |
|---|---|
| *What readers will learn* | Describe what readers will learn, and the level of expertise to be reached. |
| *What readers should know* | Describe what readers should know before they can make use of the document's information. |
| *Materials and equipment required* | Describe the materials and equipment readers need before they begin. |
| *How to set up* | Tell readers how to set up equipment or prepare materials. |

| | |
|---|---|
| *How to use document* | Tell how the document is arranged. |
| *Working definitions and conventions* | If you have five or fewer definitions, define them here. Describe the conventions (formatting, abbreviations, etc.) used in the document. |
| *Warnings and cautions* | Warn or caution readers about any pitfalls or possibilities of serious error. |
| *Theory behind process* | If necessary, explain the principle or theory behind the process. |
| *List of major steps* | Include a list of the major steps, tasks, or functions. |

THE DISCUSSION:

| | |
|---|---|
| *Procedure A, B, etc.* | Describe the purpose, special conditions, and steps in each procedure. |

THE CONCLUSION:

| | |
|---|---|
| *Review of the major steps* | Review the major steps when the instructions are lengthy or complex. |
| *Troubleshooting tips* | Tell readers how to handle potential problems. |
| *Advice for special circumstances* | Advise readers of any special conditions that may occasionally affect the instructions or affect only a small percentage of readers. |

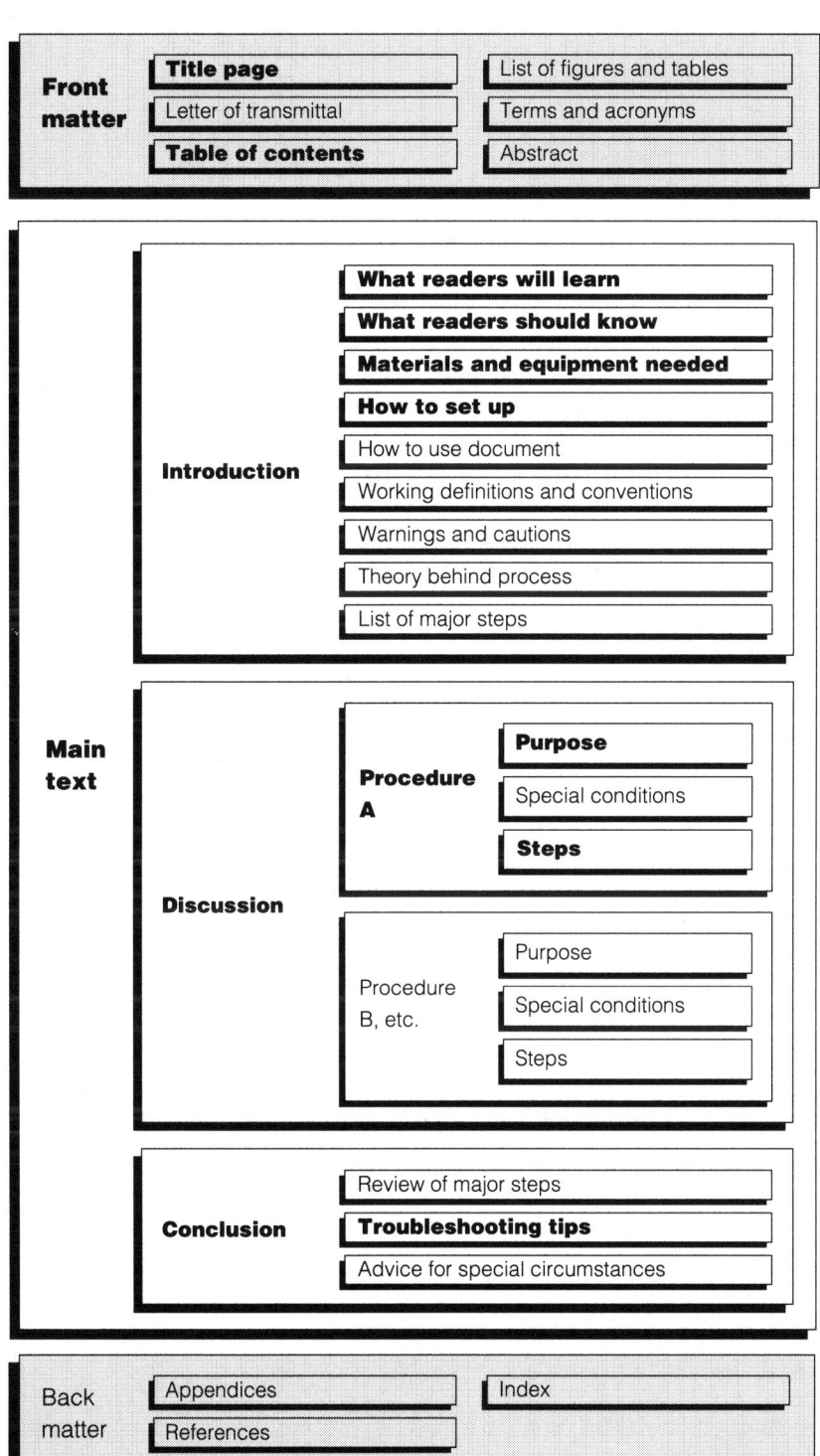

**Necessary modules**   Optional modules

**Figure 7.1.** Modules in Instructional Materials.

## CHOOSING THE RIGHT ORGANIZATION

For some instructional materials, you may need to use a type of organization different from the one described above. For example, you might have to fill the needs of more than one group of readers, or your material may be extremely complex.

In these circumstances, you can organize your material by using one or more of the following logical orders:

- ○ Chronological order
- ○ General-to-specific order
- ○ Simple-to-complex order
- ○ Order of utility

Three major types of organization in use today are worth mentioning. They are:

- ○ Tutorial
- ○ Guide to mastery
- ○ Reference

In a tutorial, the writer chooses a *scenario* (a typical task or series of tasks that accomplish a specific goal) and takes the readers through the basic steps at their lowest level from start to finish (chronological order). Tutorials are commonly written for readers who have little knowledge of the subject. For instance, if you were teaching readers soldering skills, you might start with a simple scenario that shows them how to solder an elbow joint to a piece of copper pipe.

In a guide to mastery, the writer teaches the reader how to perform each task to the degree of mastery needed (general-to-specific order). Guides to mastery are usually written for readers who have a rudimentary knowledge of the subject, sometimes learned from a tutorial.

In a reference, instead of teaching the readers how to *do* each task, the writer describes every function to its fullest, including every available option.

References are commonly written for readers with a high level of knowledge of the subject. Or they provide information readers will need only occasionally. The writer assumes that readers know what they want to do and can determine how to do it if given enough information.

The order in a reference isn't necessarily logical; it is often alphabetical.

In the sample outlines below, you'll see these three basic types of organization and how they're sometimes combined to organize instructional materials.

---

## SAMPLE OUTLINE
## FOR AN INSTRUCTION BOOKLET

---

In a simple set of instructions, you merely list the steps, beginning with the first one and proceeding in chronological order to the last one. But sometimes your readers need background information before they can begin to learn even the simplest task (order of utility). For instance, a user's guide for office management software might start with an overview of accounting principles.

For example, say you're writing a manual on how to make printed circuit boards and your readers have no prior knowledge of the subject. You want to give them basic information, enough to make a simple printed circuit board but not enough to make them experts.

The first section of the document might be an overview of circuit boards, describing the materials they're made of and the way they're classified. Then, when the readers have enough background information, you partition the tasks (general-to-specific order) into separate sections: instructions for preparing artwork, layout procedures, and so on, arranged in a chronological order.

Your outline might look like this:

    I.  INTRODUCTION
        A. What readers will learn
        B. What readers need to know
        C. Materials and equipment needed
        D. Overview
            1. Definition of a printed circuit
            2. Development of printed-circuit board
            3. Board construction and preparation (including flow
               chart of process)
        E. How to use this booklet
   II.  THE CIRCUIT BOARD
        A. Board classification
            1. Copper foil
            2. Base material
        B. General guidelines
  III.  MAKING PRINTED CIRCUIT BOARDS
        A. Artwork preparation
        B. Layout procedures
        C. Photo layout procedures
        D. Silk-screen procedures
        E. Etching the board
        F. Final processing
   IV.  A PROJECT (a practice exercise)
    V.  APPENDIX
        A. List of major suppliers of materials and equipment
   VI.  INDEX

## SAMPLE OUTLINE FOR A USER'S GUIDE

Some instructional materials combine explanation with instruction and, to meet the readers' needs, use a combination of logical orders. In this example, a fully developed outline for a manual of instructions titled *Learning Blueprint Software*, the simple-to-complex order is combined with the order of utility.

The manual uses the order of utility by giving all readers necessary background information in its introduction. The manual is divided into sections arranged in the simple-to-complex order to meet the needs of the different groups of readers, each with varying levels of technical knowledge. "Blueprint Basics" covers easy-to-learn tasks; "Advanced Blueprint Skills," harder tasks. "Technical Reference" gives complex technical detail. Information in the appendices meets the special needs of a small percentage of readers who have high-level technical knowledge. The reference section contains information that would, if it were included in the first two sections, interrupt and slow down the learning process.

MAIN TEXT
  INTRODUCTION:
    A. What you will learn in this manual
    B. How to use the manual
    C. Equipment needed
    D. What you need to know
    E. How to set up Blueprint on the computer
    F. Terms used in this manual
    G. Conventions used in this manual

DISCUSSION:
  PART I: BLUEPRINT BASICS
    A. Chapter 1: Learning Blueprint
      (Hands-on tutorial in which user creates and saves a
      basic drawing)
    B. Chapter 2: Managing Files
    C. Chapter 3: Using Drawing Tools
    D. Chapter 4: Making Revisions
    E. Chapter 5: Using Mathematical Functions
  PART II: ADVANCED BLUEPRINT SKILLS
    A. Chapter 6: Changing Drawing Perspective
    B. Chapter 7: Using a Printer or Plotter
    C. Chapter 8: Defining Colors and Patterns
    D. Chapter 9: Creating Your Own Drawing Tools
    E. Chapter 10: Writing Macros
  PART III: TECHNICAL REFERENCE
    A. Commands
    B. Error Messages
  CONCLUSION
    A. Trouble-shooting tips
    B. Using the T-200 to make slides
BACK MATTER
  APPENDICES
    A. Special Printer Adaptations
    B. Using Blueprint with Film Devices
    C. How to Remap Keys
    D. International Customization
  INDEX

Instructional materials require thoughtful planning, because the readers' needs and the document's goals can be so varied. The guidelines in this chapter should give you a start in the right direction. (Chapter 12, "Writing Instructions and Persuasive Passages," describes how to write the actual instructions.)

# CHAPTER 8

# Outlining Proposals and Promotional Materials

—Do you know the standard modules that go into a proposal?

—What are the goals of your promotional material?

—Who are the readers of your promotional material, and how can you persuade them to your point of view?

—What arrangement of modules would best suit your promotional material?

—Can you organize and outline your proposal or your promotional material using basic techniques of classification, partition, subordination and logical order?

The Superior Corporation should have won the contract. They had the most experience and could have saved the customer a lot of money. Why did they lose out? Maybe they didn't know how to put together an effective proposal. Maybe the promotional materials they'd been mailing out were duds. This chapter contains guidelines for organizing and creating proposals and promotional materials that get results.

A proposal and a promotional piece have similar goals; they're trying to sell something. The way you organize proposals, however, follows a standard pattern, whereas the way you organize promotional materials varies widely (and sometimes wildly).

## OUTLINING PROPOSALS

Most organizations and private or government agencies provide guidelines for preparing the proposals you submit to them. In these cases, you don't have to worry about organizing or outlining, you simply follow their guidelines. When the task of organizing and outlining a proposal falls on your shoulders, follow the guidelines in this chapter.

### STANDARD MODULES IN A PROPOSAL

All proposals, whether simple or complex, have a standard organization as shown in Figure 8.1. The front matter and back matter contain the standard modules found in most documents. (You can see examples of them in Chapter 16.)

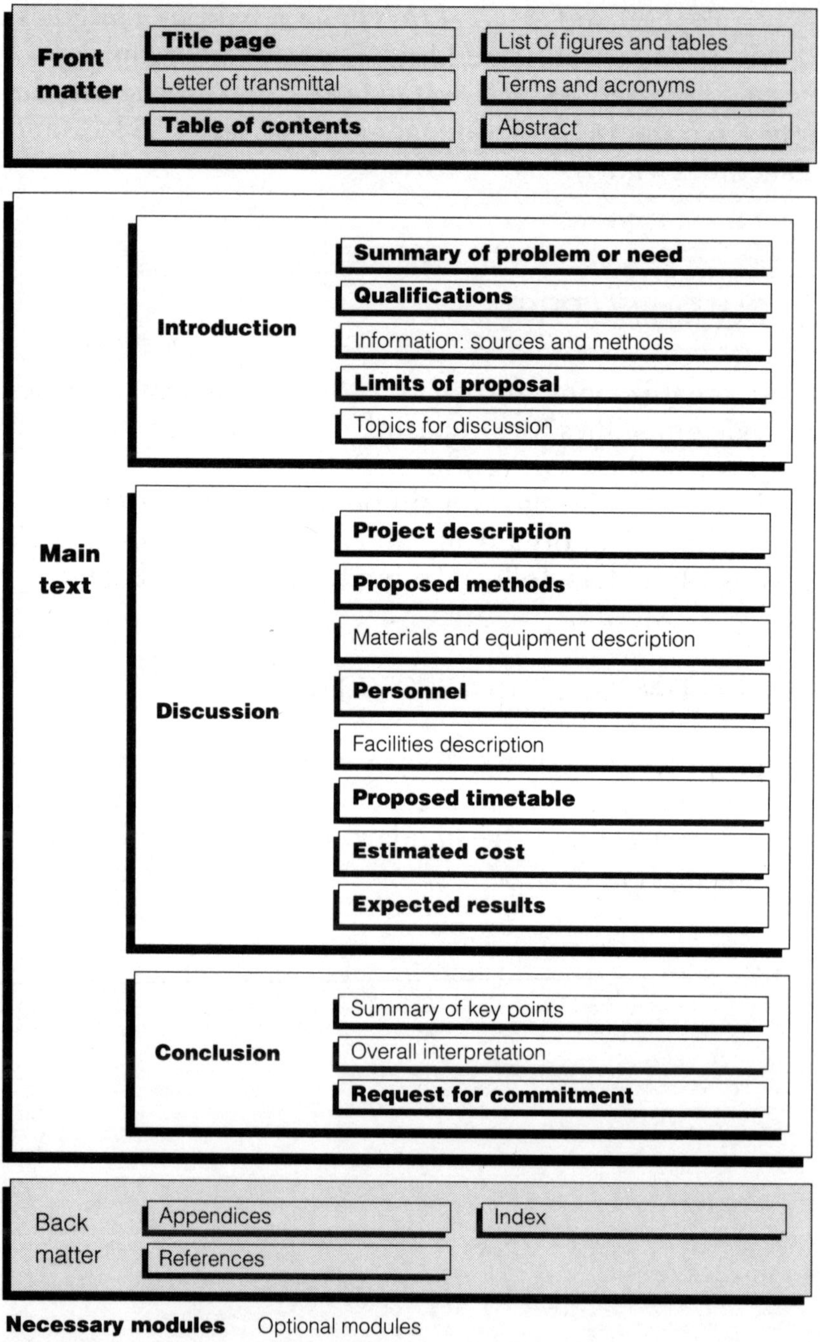

**Front matter**

| Title page | List of figures and tables |
| Letter of transmittal | Terms and acronyms |
| Table of contents | Abstract |

**Main text**

Introduction
- Summary of problem or need
- Qualifications
- Information: sources and methods
- Limits of proposal
- Topics for discussion

Discussion
- Project description
- Proposed methods
- Materials and equipment description
- Personnel
- Facilities description
- Proposed timetable
- Estimated cost
- Expected results

Conclusion
- Summary of key points
- Overall interpretation
- Request for commitment

**Back matter**

| Appendices | Index |
| References | |

**Necessary modules**   Optional modules

**Figure 8.1.** Modules in a Proposal.

The main text, as in all technical documents, contains an introduction, a discussion, and a conclusion.

*THE INTRODUCTION:*

| | |
|---|---|
| *Summary of problem or need* | Sum up the problem or the need as briefly as possible. |
| *Qualifications* | Describe the organization's (or the individual's) qualifications, including recommendations, endorsements, past successes. |
| *Methods used to gather information, or sources of information* | Explain how you got the information you're using in the proposal. |
| *Limits of proposal* | Describe exactly what the proposal will and will not cover. |
| *Topics for discussion* | List the topics the proposal will cover. |

*THE DISCUSSION:*

| | |
|---|---|
| *Project description* | Start with an overview of the proposed project. |
| *Proposed methods* | Describe the methods you will use to carry out the project. |
| *Description of materials and equipment* | Describe the materials and the equipment to be used in the project. |

| | |
|---|---|
| *Personnel* | Give the number and qualifications of the personnel who will work on the project. |
| *Description of facilities* | Describe the facilities (space, offices, buildings) needed to complete the project. |
| *Proposed timetable* | Propose a schedule for completion of the project. |
| *Estimated cost* | Tell the readers what the product or service, as described, will cost them. |
| *Expected results* | Describe the specifics of how the product will perform or what the service will do. |

THE CONCLUSION:

| | |
|---|---|
| *Summary* | Summarize the key points. |
| *Request for commitment* | Ask the readers to sign on the dotted line. |

## SAMPLE OUTLINE FOR A SIMPLE PROPOSAL

The discussion in a simple proposal will contain the modules described above but will differ in the depth of the information you present. For instance, in a complex proposal, you might divide the module "Project Description" into several topics, each with many subtopics. In a simple proposal, you might be able to cover "Project Description" with two or three paragraphs.

The following outline is for a proposal by an independent consultant to conduct an efficiency study for a manufacturing firm.

I. Introduction
   A. Statement of problem: Rising costs in industry
   B. TimeSavers, Inc. qualifications
      1. Nine years of experience
      2. Small Business of the Year, 1969, 1973, 1979, 1982, 1988
      3. Testimonials from clients
II. Discussion
   A. Methods for study
      1. Observation in three areas
         a. Efficiency of equipment
         b. Efficiency of personnel and work methods
         c. Efficiency of scheduling process
      2. Interviews with selected managers and employees
   B. Total time frame: Two weeks
      1. Three days observation at plant
      2. Two days interviews at plant
      3. One day additional observation (optional after interviews)
      4. Five working days to complete and deliver report
      5. Scheduled either the last two weeks of September or the first two weeks of November
   C. Personnel who will conduct interviews
      1. Lead (15 years experience)
      2. Two interviewers (total 7 years experience)
   D. Report will contain:
      1. Summary of observations
      2. Summary of interviews
      3. Statement of existing or potential areas for improvement
      4. Recommendation for improving production
         a. List of suggested improvements
         b. Plan for implementing changes
   E. Cost of study
   F. Expected results
      1. Increased efficiency in production with resulting savings of between 10 and 17 percent
III. Conclusion
   A. Summary
      1. Benefits of study substantial
      2. Cost of study regained in three months savings
      3. Can conduct study unobtrusively, not upset employees or schedule
   B. Would like to schedule study by July 1

## SAMPLE OUTLINE FOR A COMPLEX PROPOSAL

The next example is a proposal to build an Antarctic scientific research camp, a much larger project than the one we discussed in the last example. The government agency in charge of this project provided specific directions for the format of the proposal and general specifications for the research camp. The agency wanted a description of what the company would deliver but not a description of their methods.

MAIN TEXT
  I. INTRODUCTION
    A. General description of project
    B. BestBild Corporation's qualifications
      1. Twenty years of experience
      2. List of major projects
      3. Copies of letters of recommendation
    C. Scope of proposal
  II. PROJECT DESCRIPTION
    A. General description of camp
    B. Site
      1. Description of landscape
      2. Description of climate
      3. Proximity to harbor
    C. Proposed building layout
      1. Living quarters
      2. Cafeteria/kitchen
      3. Laboratories
      4. Recreation area
      5. Infirmary
      6. Storage huts
      7. Power plant
      8. Fuel depot
    D. Proposed utilities plan
      1. Electrical system
        a. Heating
        b. Lighting
        c. Primary system control
        d. Backup system control
      2. Solar collector system

        3. Plumbing system
           a. Fresh water system
           b. Waste disposal field
        4. Trash incinerator
     E. Circulation and transportation plan
        1. Dock at harbor
        2. Road to harbor
        3. Helicopter landing pad
        4. Walkways between buildings
           a. Covered walkways
           b. Tunnels
III. Personnel
     A. Supervisors and consultants
        1. Number
        2. Experience
     B. Crew
        1. Number
        2. Experience
IV. Facilities
     A. Available
     B. Needed
 V. Cost analysis
     A. Transportation/and temporary housing for building
       crew
     B. Construction of buildings
     C. Walkways between buildings
     D. Helicopter landing pad
     E. Dock and roadway to dock
     F. Removal of temporary crew quarters
VI. Timetable
     A. Final blueprints and specifications prepared
     B. Temporary crew quarters established
     C. Dock and roadway to dock completed
     D. Helicopter landing pad completed
     E. Buildings completed
     F. Walkways between buildings completed
     G. Removal of temporary crew quarters
VII. CONCLUSION
     A. Summary of qualifications and benefits
     B. Request for contract

## OUTLINING PROMOTIONAL MATERIALS

Promotional materials include letters, direct-mail pieces, advertisements, or brochures, each one a document whose goal is to sell a product or service. Like studies and research reports, promotional materials inform and educate, and like recommendation reports, they use persuasive tactics.

### STANDARD MODULES IN PROMOTIONAL MATERIALS

Promotional pieces usually contain front matter, main text, and back matter as shown in Figure 8.2.

*MODULES IN FRONT MATTER*

| | |
|---|---|
| *Title* | Choose a title to get the readers' attention or arouse their curiosity. (*Do You Know How to Double Your Sales?*) |
| *Name of company* | Identify company, including affiliations and credentials. |
| *Leading statement* | Hook the readers and make them want to read on. Often you can use a leading question. (*How many times did you have to call a service technician last year?*) |

*MODULES IN MAIN TEXT*

*Introduction:*

| | |
|---|---|
| *Overview of need* | Give an overview describing the need for the product or service. |

| | |
|---|---|
| *Overview of how needs can be met* | Give an overview of how the product or service meets the need. |
| *Description of qualifications* | Describe the company's or the individual's qualifications, which might be a list of endorsements, recommendations, or successful projects. |

*Discussion:*

| | |
|---|---|
| *Benefits* | Describe the benefits of your product or service. |

*Conclusion:*

| | |
|---|---|
| *Summary of benefits* | Give the readers a final sell. |
| *Options or technical information* | Tell readers about the options or describe other technical information they need to help them make up their minds. |
| *Contact information* | Tell the readers how to order, where to write, or who to call for more information. |

*MODULES IN THE BACK MATTER:*

*Company name*

*Company phone number and address*

*Company logo*

The front matter in your promotional material might be the cover page of a brochure or a direct-mail piece, or it could be the introduction to an article. The back matter might be the back page of a brochure or a direct-mail piece, or the conclusion to an article.

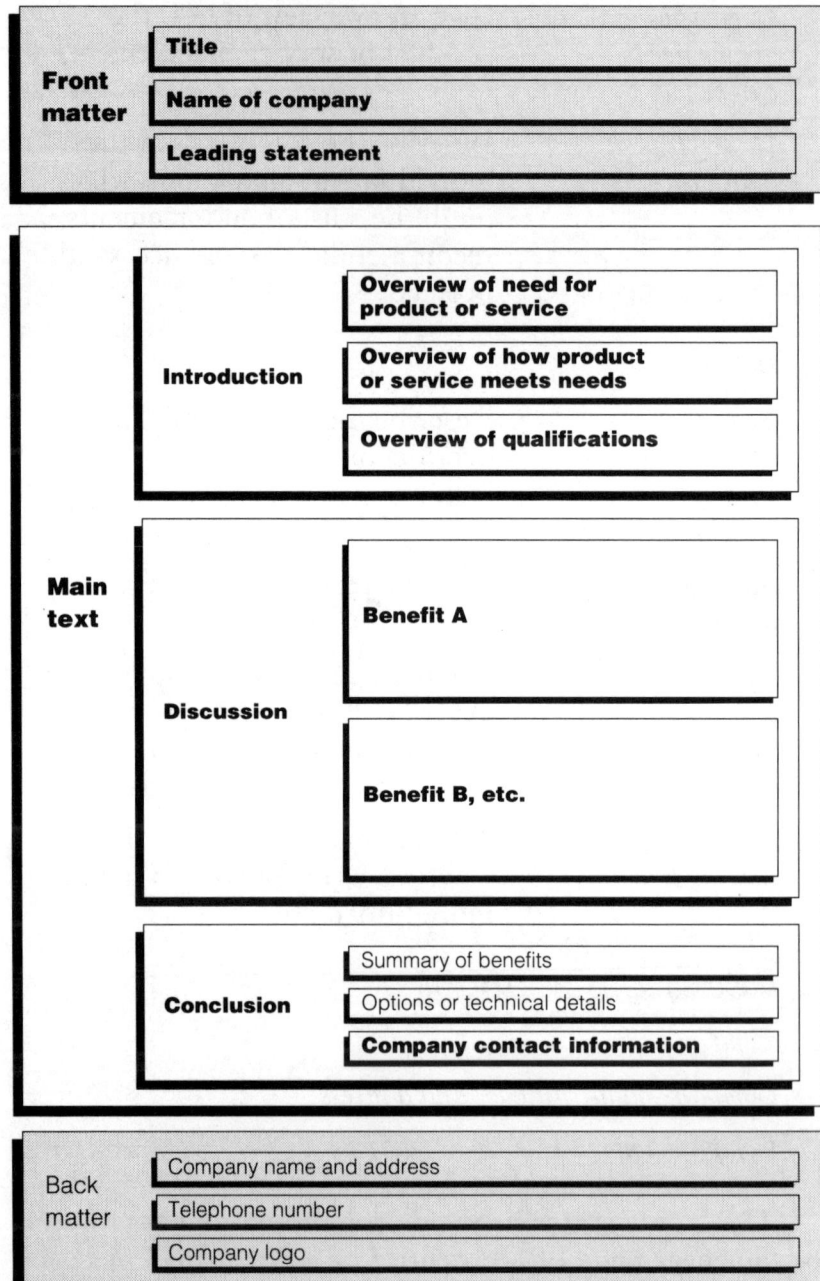

**Necessary modules**    Optional modules

**Figure 8.2.** Modules in Promotional Material.

## ORGANIZING PROMOTIONAL MATERIALS

One way to organize a promotional piece is to structure it the way you would a recommendation report (Figure 8.3). With this organization, you describe so many marvelous and specific attributes that the readers cannot escape drawing the conclusion that your product or service is superior (specific-to-general order).

You can also make effective use of the compare-and-contrast order, the order of importance, and the order of utility in promotional material.

## SAMPLE OUTLINE FOR A PROMOTIONAL FLYER

Occasionally, you'll actually take a research report or study and adapt it to serve as a promotional piece. As an example, say you want to send out a "news bulletin" to promote a new drug for arthritis sufferers. The goals of the document are to inform the readers about the drug and promote its sale.

The readers of this promotional piece would be physicians and pharmacists. The physicians who specialize in arthritis have a high level of technical knowledge about the subject. Other physicians and pharmacists may not. The specialists need more technical information about your drug and its usefulness than the other readers. On the other hand, the other readers need general information about the symptoms of arthritis.

To meet the needs of the less knowledgeable readers, you can use the order of utility by including background material on arthritis. In a promotional piece, you can use a *sidebar* (a boxed-off, short article tucked into your main text). The more knowledgeable readers can easily skip the information in the sidebar. (For a report, you might add an appendix.)

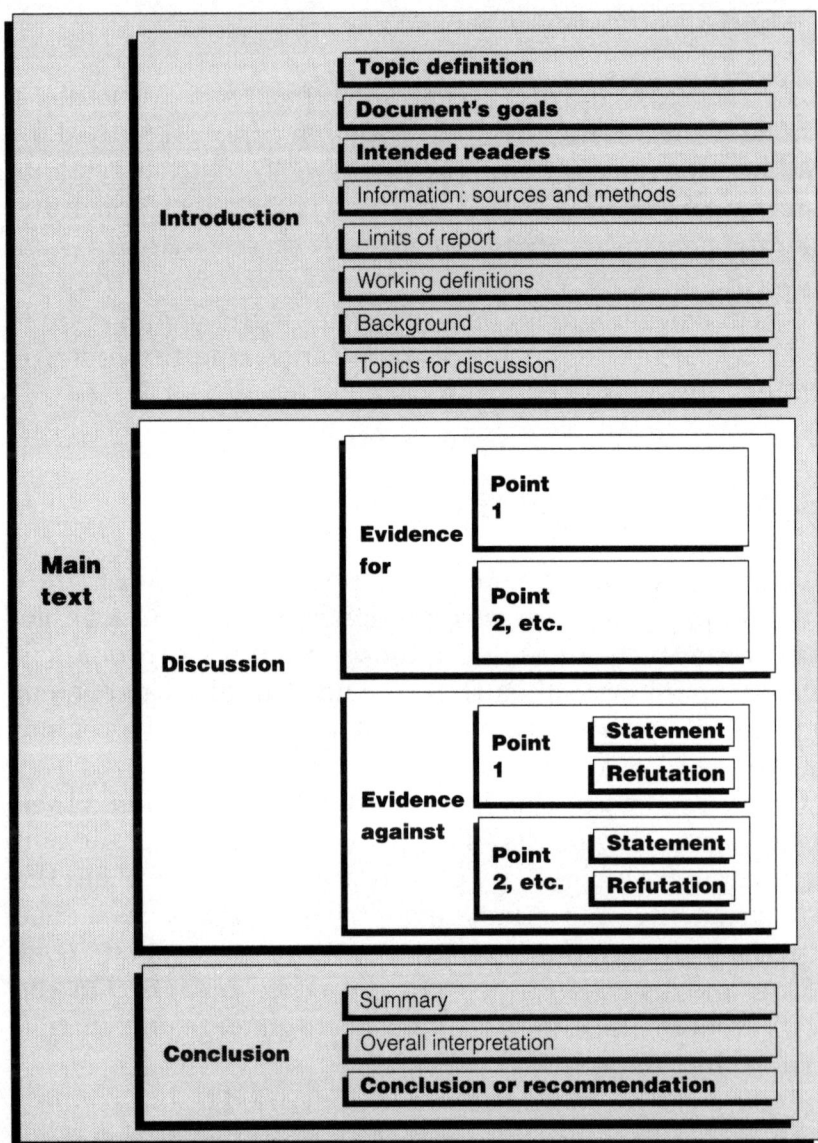

**Figure 8.3.** Discussion Modules in a Recommendation Report.

The points you need to make in the document are:

○ Our lab has developed a new drug for the relief of arthritis symptoms.

○ This drug is better than others now on the market.

○ We have developed and tested this drug in a thorough, scientific manner.

○ We can reliably predict this drug's effects on patients.

○ This drug is not for all arthritis patients, and doctors should use it according to our guidelines.

Your preliminary outline might look like the following:

   I. Introduction
     A. Topic statement
     B. Description of research methods
     C. Overview of drug's benefits
  II. Discussion
     A. First benefit
       1. Definition
       2. Description
       3. Why it is more beneficial than other drugs
     B. Second benefit, etc.
       1. Definition
       2. Description
       3. Why it is more beneficial than other drugs
 III. Conclusion
     A. Summary of benefits
     B. Summary of how drug is better than other drugs (with table)
     C. Recommendations for using drug
 IV. Sidebar
     A. Overview of arthritis

At this point, you might want to look over your outline to see whether or not you covered all points you need to make. Will this document accomplish your goals? Meet your readers' needs? The physicians who specialize in arthritis need more detailed technical information on the drug. Another sidebar could easily fill this need.

## SAMPLE OUTLINE FOR A PROMOTIONAL PAMPHLET

This outline uses the compare-and-contrast order in an alternatives analysis type of structure to show how your product or service is better than the competition's product or service. Figure 8.4 diagrams the modules in this type of organization.

Often, you will combine the compare-and-contrast order with the specific-to-general order in your promotional pieces. As an example, say that you're writing a pamphlet to promote a commercial vacuum cleaner to potential customers. Your goal is to inspire readers to purchase your company's vacuum cleaner instead of your competitors' vacuum cleaners. To accomplish this goal, you need to give the readers evidence that your product will fill their needs. Use the specific-to-general order to list the evidence before concluding that your company's product is best.

You have these points to make about your vacuum cleaner. It is

- more durable than the competition's vacuum cleaner.
- easier to handle.
- more compact in size.
- a better performer.
- worth its higher cost.

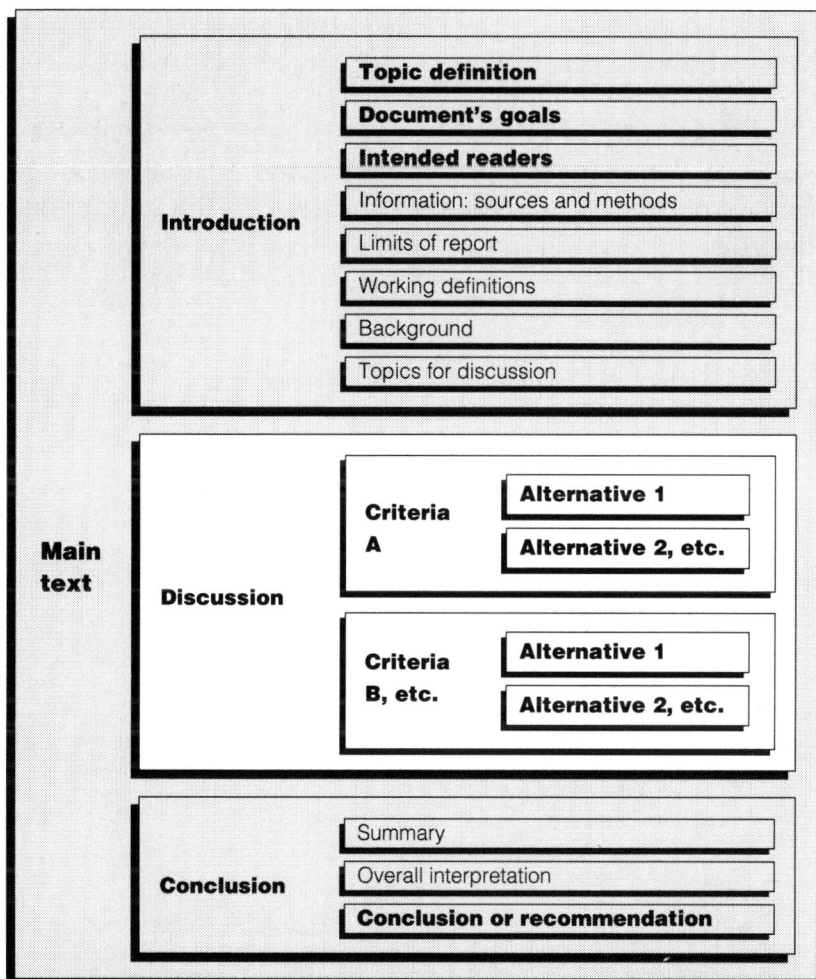

**Figure 8.4.**  Discussion Modules in an Alternatives Analysis.

You then use these criteria to compare and contrast your product with the products of your major competitors. You should have the results of several tests from which to draw this information. (We discuss how to write persuasive passages in detail in Chapter 12, "Writing Instructions and Persuasive Passages.") Your preliminary outline might look like this:

I. Introduction
   A. Statement introducing product
   B. Background information on company
   C. Background or history of product
   D. Description of how tests were carried out
   E. List of selling points
II. Discussion
   A. Durability
      1. Your product
      2. Competitor 1
      3. Competitor 2
   B. Easy handling
      1. Your product, etc.
      2. Competitor 1
      3. Competitor 2
   C. Compact size
      1. Your product, etc.
   D. Performance
      1. Your product, etc.
   E. Cost
      1. Your product, etc.
III. Conclusion
   A. Summary of selling points
   B. Conclusion that your product is best
   C. Recommendation to choose product

## SAMPLE OUTLINE FOR A PROMOTIONAL BROCHURE

Here's an outline for a promotional brochure that will be sent out by direct mail to a mailing list of potential customers. The writer assumes that readers interested in modems would have at least a rudimentary knowledge of computers. The writer presents evidence to convince the readers that this modem is the best on the market (specific-to-general order). Evidence is arranged in order of descending importance, because a direct mail piece has to catch attention fast. In a longer piece, the writer might catch the reader's attention by hinting at a startling new development, then arranging the evidence in order of ascending importance with the clincher at the end.

   I. Meet the RPM-7000 Series Radioteleprinter Modem, which is virtually error-free, fast, and flexible.
  II. Why can we make these claims?
    A. Our modem reduces errors in transmission
      1. Operates through 4-second circuit outages and noise bursts
      2. Transmits or receives any binary code: synchronous or asynchronous, clear or encrypted data
      3. Employs 7-fold time and frequency redundancy
    B. Transmits and receives at speeds up to 110 baud
    C. Continually reports circuit conditions
    D. Interfaces with a variety of teleprinters
 III. Summary of points
 IV. Summary of technical specifications
  V. Back matter
    A. Company logo, address, and phone number for more information

Organizing and outlining proposals, whether simple or complex, is easy once you know what modules to include. And once you know about the wide variety of techniques you can choose from to organize promotional materials, they are a lot more fun to write.

# PART THREE

# WRITING YOUR DOCUMENT

# CHAPTER 9

# Building Modules with Paragraphs and Passages

WRITING SOLID PARAGRAPHS

LINKING IDEAS WITH TRANSITIONS

ARRANGING DETAILS IN LOGICAL ORDER

WRITING HELPFUL HEADINGS

MAKING MATERIAL EASY TO DIGEST

—Do you introduce your topic in the first sentence of a paragraph, follow it up with supporting information, and then summarize it?

—Do you link sentences and paragraphs with transitions?

—Do you arrange information in a logical order?

—Do your headings help readers find their way around in your document?

—Do you arrange information into short and easy-to-read paragraphs?

—Do you arrange series of items into easy-to-follow lists?

After you complete your preparations and outline your document, the fun part begins; it's time to sit down and write. In this chapter, we describe how to build modules from the ground up. We describe how to write solid paragraphs and passages using basic composition techniques such as topic sentences, transitions, and logical orders. We also describe how to write helpful headings, and how to arrange material with short paragraphs and lists so that it is easy to read.

## WRITING SOLID PARAGRAPHS

In Chapter 1, "Technical Documents and Their Modules," we described how to organize the major sections of a technical document. For instance, the three major modules of the main text are the introduction, the discussion, and the conclusion. This "three-part" method is also an effective tool for organizing information into solid, well-constructed paragraphs.

When you introduce a new topic for discussion:

1. State your topic in the first sentence of your new paragraph.

2. Present information to support the topic.

3. Summarize the information or conclude the discussion. Simple topics, however, may not require a conclusion. But when you have a point to make or your discussion is complex, be sure to sum up for the readers.

Figure 9.1 illustrates the modules of a simple paragraph.

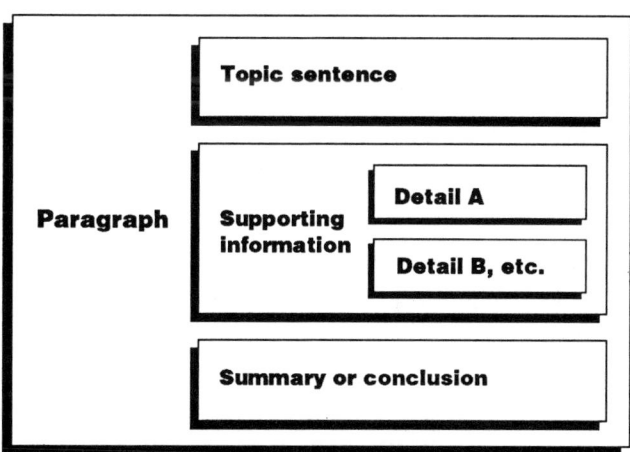

**Figure 9.1.** Paragraph Covering a Simple Topic.

In this module from a recommendation report, the topic definition is in the introduction. So that you can see its structure, we have broken down the paragraph into its separate sentences.

| | |
|---|---|
| *Topic sentence* | Baldwin Engineering has a better way to balance horizontal reciprocating forces in compressors. |
| *Support* | Our method is old, simple, and reliable. |
| *Support* | Most companies balance horizontal reciprocating forces by using counterweights. |
| *Support* | Baldwin Engineering balances straight-path reciprocating forces with straight-path reciprocating forces. |
| *Support* | We accomplish this by mounting cylinders on opposite sides of the crank-case. |
| *Support* | Crank throws are phased 180 degrees apart so that piston motions are equal and opposite. |
| *Support* | Obviously, if the reciprocating weights on each side are equal, there is no unbalanced force trying to move the entire compressor horizontally. |
| *Conclusion* | Baldwin Engineering's way is simple, and better. |

The topic sentence makes a claim and the supporting sentences amplify, compare, and present details to back up the claim (general-to-specific order).

## COVERING COMPLEX TOPICS

In the example above, one paragraph happened to be enough to cover the topic. However, many topics will need more supporting information than you can cover in only one paragraph. For example, you might organize the discussion of a complex topic this way:

1. The first paragraph begins with the topic sentence and then lists the points that the discussion covers.

2. The second and following paragraphs contain supporting information, each supporting paragraph covering one of the points listed in the first paragraph.

3. The final paragraph contains the summary or conclusion.

Figure 9.2 illustrates this type of organization. The most important guidelines to remember are:

O Announce your topics to your readers.

O Let your readers know when your discussion of the topic is over, especially when the discussion is lengthy or complex.

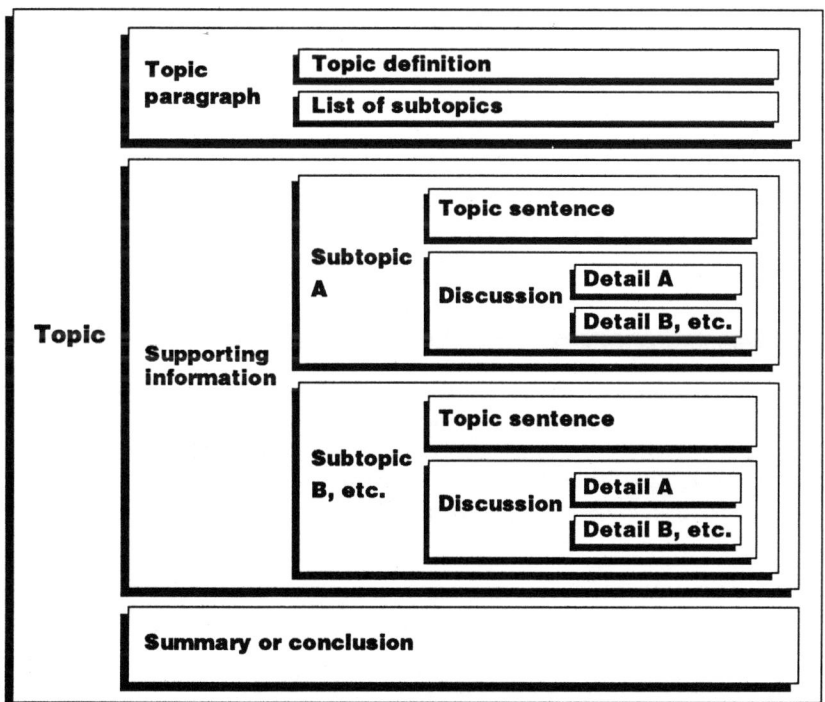

**Figure 9.2.** Module Covering a Complex Topic.

## LINKING IDEAS WITH TRANSITIONS

Keeping readers on track when you move from one idea to the next or from one topic to a new one can be a challenge. *Transitions*, which express relationships between one idea and another, help readers follow your train of thought. They tell the readers that you're changing the topic, or saying more about the topic, or showing a contrast, and so on.

Mark a path for your readers by making liberal use of transitional devices such as:

O  Transitional words and phrases.

O  Repetition of key words and phrases.

O  Parallel grammatical construction.

### TRANSITIONAL WORDS AND PHRASES

We use transitional words and phrases in sentences and paragraphs all the time with such words as *and, if, also,* and *another way.* As you can see in the following example, a paragraph can sound blunt and graceless without them.

*Without Transitions*

You can create macros that automatically open menus, issue commands, and place applications in windows. You can optimize the program's performance by specifying how much processing time each application receives. You cannot direct it to automatically load specific programs.

In the revised paragraph, two simple transitional words ease the flow of ideas for the readers and make the relationships clear.

*With Transitions*

You can create macros that automatically open menus, issue commands, and place applications in windows. You can *also* optimize the performance by specifying how much processing time each application receives. *However*, you cannot direct it to automatically load specific programs.

Here are some of the most useful words and phrases for linking sentences and paragraphs:

| | | |
|---|---|---|
| if | for example | another way |
| because | for instance | once |
| unless | after | additionally |
| but | before | similarly |
| however | therefore | now |
| then | until | later |
| formerly | instead | otherwise |
| next | also | |

The use of these and other words and phrases make it easy for the readers to follow your thoughts. The following example illustrates.

*Transitional Words and Phrases*

... *For this reason* you must keep the board moving in the tank. You should *also* keep the liquid etchant moving. Once the etchant reacts with the copper, the chemical action reduces its effectiveness. *Therefore*, you want the board to be continuously in contact with fresh etchant. *One way* to do this is to use the rocking tray as described above.

*Another way* to keep the etchant moving is to ...

## TRANSITIONAL PARAGRAPHS

When you're dealing with several major topic modules, transitional paragraphs can guide readers from one topic to the next. Often this transitional paragraph summarizes or concludes the current topic and then announces the new topic. As an example, here's a transitional paragraph that ties two modules together.

> The preceding section outlined the conditions necessary for symbiosis. Now, we need to discuss exactly how to duplicate these conditions.

## REPETITION OF KEY WORDS AND PHRASES

Repetition of key words and phrases is another useful device for linking ideas. One simple way to do this is to conclude a paragraph by listing the points that the subsequent passages will cover. The following example is the beginning of a topic module in a research report. The first sentence defines the topic and announces the two subtopics.

*REPETITION OF KEY WORDS*

|  |  |
|---|---|
|  | As an example of how construction details can differ in sanitary wells drilled in consolidated formations, consider these two |
| *Key word (1)* | types of water-bearing rocks: *sandstone*, |
| *Key words (2)* | which has small pores, and the *limestone and basalt* type, which has crevices and fractures. |
| *Repetition (1)* | In *sandstone*, water moves through small pores similar to the pores in an unconsolidated sand formation. The size of the openings is usually small enough to effectively filter the water as it moves into and through the acquifer. |
| *Repetition (2)* | In *limestone and basalt*, water moves ... |

Or you may simply repeat a word or phrase to keep readers focused on the topic, as in this example, which is the subtopic definition module in a research report:

*REPETITION OF KEY WORD OR PHRASE*

| | |
|---|---|
| *Topic* | This section covers the *infectious agents* in those diseases that cause arthritis by the direct invasion of the microorganism into the joint. |
| *Repetition* | The *infectious agent* may be a bacterium, a virus, or a fungus; you can usually remove it from the synovial fluid or the synovial membrane. This means that you can generally use a specific treatment. |
| *Repetition* | Most of the *infectious agents* arrive at the joint via the blood stream. |

## PARALLEL CONSTRUCTION

*Parallel construction* is the repetition of grammatical structure in tense, voice, and placement of phrases. Famous orators have made use of parallel construction, as in Winston Churchill's "We shall fight . . ." speech: "We shall fight in France, we shall fight on the seas and oceans, we shall fight with growing confidence and growing strength in the air, we shall . . ."

The simplest and most common use of parallel construction is in passages that contain a series. For instance, each item in the following series has the same pattern and begins with a verb.

Once you establish the pattern, you can *copy* the design, *save* time and money, *improve* training procedures, and *instill* confidence in the operators.

You can use parallel construction to link ideas within a paragraph, and also to link two or more separate paragraphs.

To use parallel construction to link paragraphs, begin each paragraph with a sentence that uses the same tense, voice, and placement of phrases. In the simple example below, the prepositional phrase beginning with the word *in* at the beginning of each paragraph lets the readers know that the second paragraph is also about the "Kirchhoff flow."

> *In principle*, you can determine the two-dimensional Kirchhoff flow over a polygonal obstacle by constructing a conformal map onto a polygon in the log-hodograph plane.
>
> *In practice*, however, . . .

Here's another example; it uses an *if* phrase to link ideas.

> *If the water level falls below the FULL point but stays above the HALF point*, the stacks are in no danger and personnel can proceed with business as usual. The water level normally stays at FULL and will rarely fall below the HALF point.
>
> *If the lubricating fluid level falls below the FULL point*, some precautions should be taken to protect the stacks and the personnel, even though there is still no danger. The lubricating fluid level will rarely fall this far; fail-safe measures and switches at three different levels would have to stop functioning.
>
> *If the gas level falls below the FULL point*, the situation is . . .

Transitions can make the difference between a document that's easy to understand and one that's difficult and frustrating.

## ARRANGING DETAILS IN LOGICAL ORDER

Chapter 5, "Basics of Outlining" describes how to use logical orders to arrange the topics in your document. Use logical orders to organize the details in your document as well.

Table 9.1 summarizes the logical orders and how they are most commonly used.

The next few sections in this chapter cover the logical orders that give the most trouble to writers: chronological order, order of importance, and order of utility. You'll find more examples in Chapter 12, "Writing Instructions and Persuasive Passages," and Chapter 13, "Defining, Describing, and Explaining."

### USING CHRONOLOGICAL ORDER

Use chronological order to arrange procedures and descriptions of processes. Here's an example of a description of a process that is not in chronological order, but should be.

*Lacking Logical Order*

Field Procedure:

Cruisers estimate the scaling diameter of each log from a Douglas fir tree either by sight or by using an appropriate taper table. For grading purposes, they may segment thirty-two-foot logs into two sixteen-foot logs. When they grade the trees, they first decide whether the tree is old-growth or second-growth and then measure the d.b.h. and height in standard log lengths.

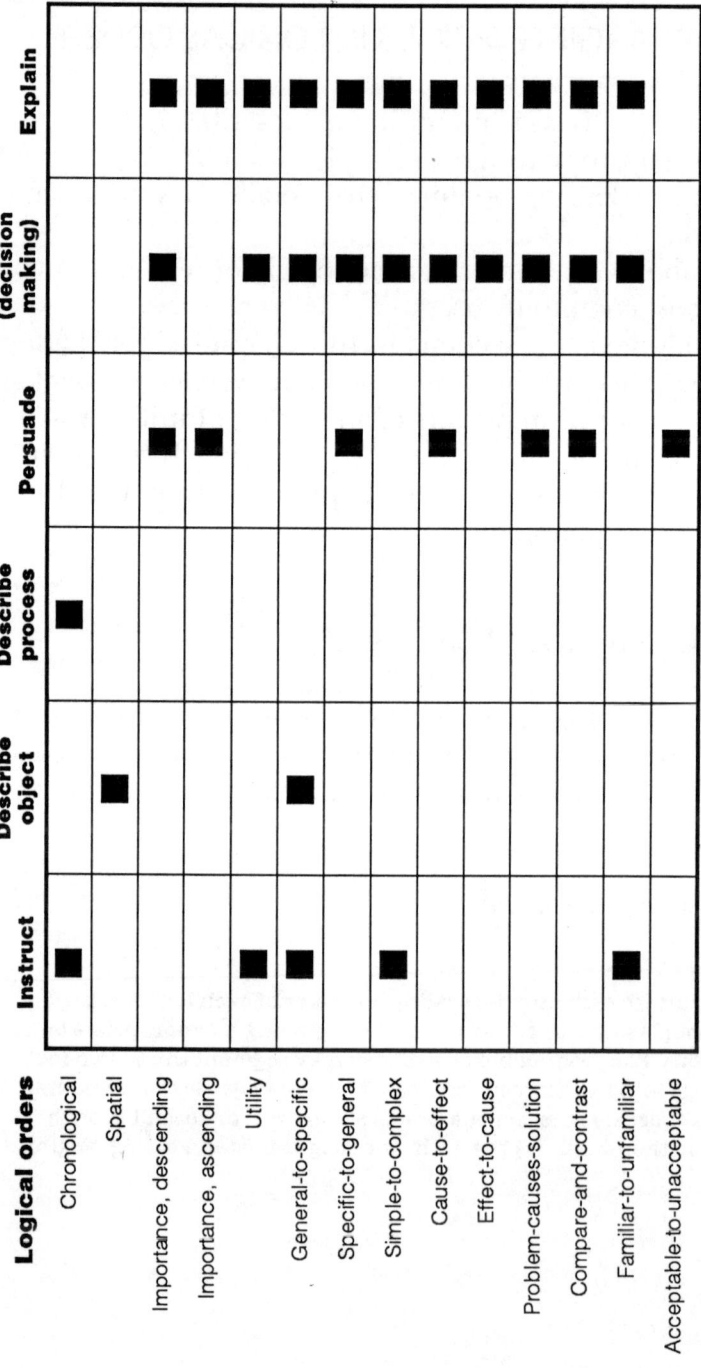

| Logical orders | Instruct | Describe object | Describe process | Persuade | Analyze (decision making) | Explain |
|---|---|---|---|---|---|---|
| Chronological | ■ | | ■ | | | |
| Spatial | | ■ | | | | |
| Importance, descending | | | | ■ | ■ | ■ |
| Importance, ascending | | | | ■ | | ■ |
| Utility | ■ | | | | | ■ |
| General-to-specific | ■ | ■ | | | | ■ |
| Specific-to-general | | | | ■ | ■ | ■ |
| Simple-to-complex | ■ | | | | ■ | ■ |
| Cause-to-effect | | | | ■ | ■ | ■ |
| Effect-to-cause | | | | | ■ | ■ |
| Problem-causes-solution | | | | ■ | ■ | ■ |
| Compare-and-contrast | | | | ■ | ■ | ■ |
| Familiar-to-unfamiliar | ■ | | | | ■ | ■ |
| Acceptable-to-unacceptable | | | | ■ | | |

**Table 9.1.**  Common Uses for Logical Orders.

Here's the same paragraph rearranged in chronological order so that it's much clearer and easier to follow.

*Using Chronological Order*

Field Procedure:

When grading Douglas fir trees, cruisers first decide whether the tree is old-growth or second-growth, and then measure the d.b.h. and height in standard log lengths. Next, the cruisers segment thirty-two foot logs into two sixteen-foot logs. They then estimate the scaling diameter of each log either by sight or by using an appropriate taper table.

## USING THE ORDER OF IMPORTANCE

The order of *descending* importance is helpful in alternatives analyses or feasibility studies, where decision makers need to know the decisive factors as soon as possible.

The order of *ascending* importance helps make a dramatic point or hold the reader's attention, as in a persuasive passage. For instance, you can greatly improve the following example from a recommendation report by rearranging the information in order of ascending importance.

*Lacks Logical Order*

As far as performance is concerned, *EasyTalk*'s general operation leaves a lot to be desired. In nonprotocol transfers, for example, it was nearly three times slower than *CommPlus*. NSTL tests show that, compared with *Proline* and *CommPlus*, some *EasyTalk* transfers were downright sluggish.

Here is the same paragraph rewritten so that the fact that will most impress the readers appears at the very end.

*Using the Order of Ascending Importance*

As far as performance is concerned, *EasyTalk*'s general operation leaves a lot to be desired. NSTL tests show that, compared with *Proline* and *CommPlus*, some *EasyTalk* transfers were downright sluggish. In nonprotocol transfers, for example, it was nearly three times slower than *CommPlus*.

You can see that the revised paragraph has more persuasive impact.

## USING THE ORDER OF UTILITY

Sometimes readers won't understand your explanation or description unless you give them some background information first.

In the following example, readers may miss the significance of the new information because an important fact is out of order.

*Lacks Logical Order*

Ultrarapid cooling has succeeded in making two metals superconducting that were previously not superconducting either alone or when alloyed in a normal manner. Frances Smythe-Jones and Pe Chu Win of the California Institute of Technology created the new alloy by cooling a molten mixture of gold and germanium at a rate of more than four million degrees Fahrenheit per second. Only a few metals and alloys exhibit the property of *superconductivity* (the complete disappearance of electrical resistance at temperatures close to absolute zero).

Because you give the readers the background information first in the following version, the significance of the information is more apparent.

*Using the Order of Utility*

Only a few metals and alloys exhibit the property of *superconductivity* (the complete disappearance of electrical resistance at temperatures close to absolute zero). Ultrarapid cooling has succeeded in making two metals superconducting that were previously not superconducting either alone or when alloyed in a normal manner. Frances Smythe-Jones and Pe Chu Win of the California Institute of Technology created the new alloy by cooling a molten mixture of gold and germanium at a rate of more than four million degrees Fahrenheit per second.

## WRITING HELPFUL HEADINGS

Headings act as signposts; they stand out boldly in the text, announcing specific topics to readers. Here are some guidelines to help you write headings:

○ Use headings whenever they are needed, to announce first-level topics, second-level topics, and, if necessary, third-level topics.

○ Use at least two second-level headings under a first-level heading if you are going to classify or partition the topic at all. This guideline also applies to third-level headings.

○ Make your headings specific and concrete; avoid vague generalities, whimsy, or cuteness.

○ Keep your headings brief, whenever possible. A brief heading is easier to read, but clarity comes first. Never sacrifice clarity for brevity.

○ If possible, make your headings consistent. For example, when one heading includes a gerund, such as "Saving the File," make all headings gerunds ("Backing up the Disk," "Making Copies of the File," etc.). However, specific and helpful headings are more important than consistency; don't try to force headings into a pattern that doesn't help readers locate information.

When you've written several pages of text under a first- or second-level heading, look back over the lengthy passages and see whether the information falls naturally into classifications or partitions. Add the necessary headings so that readers can quickly find the information they need.

Sometimes, writers are tempted to sacrifice clarity in an attempt to be "user-friendly." Resist this temptation. For example, the heading "Emergency Shutdown Procedure" is much more helpful to readers than the heading "Oh No!"

Occasionally, you'll be forced to lump information about several topics under one heading. In these instances, it's better to write a heading that's specific—even if it's a little awkward—than one that's too broad. For instance, "Backing up Tapes and Locking Machines" provides more information than "Security Measures."

## MAKING MATERIAL EASY TO DIGEST

Try to arrange material in short chunks of information that readers can easily assimilate. Use short paragraphs, arrange series of items into lists whenever possible, and make sure you arrange procedures and instructions into enumerated lists.

## WRITING SHORT PARAGRAPHS

You should keep your paragraphs short. They are easier to read and less intimidating than long paragraphs. A page full of unbroken text can be overwhelming to readers.

Short paragraphs are more attractive, adding white space to your page. They're easier to find, too, when readers look back through the document to locate a particular piece of information.

If you've written a lengthy paragraph, read it again. You'll almost certainly find that there are natural places to break it, that it contains subtopics that deserve their own paragraphs.

## LISTING INFORMATION

You can make procedures and instructions easier to follow when you arrange them in enumerated (numbered or lettered) lists. Chapter 12, "Writing Instructions and Persuasive Passages," describes how to write instructions in detail. You can also make series of related facts or details easier to read when you itemize them in lists with bullets or numbers instead of burying them in a solid paragraph.

Some of the benefits you gain by using lists are:

○ Individual emphasis makes each item more memorable.

○ Items are easier to find when readers refer back to the list later.

○ The pages in your document are easier on the eyes because lists add variety and white space.

For example, see how the following series of items seems buried in the block of prose.

*Series in a Paragraph*

Files that are not ASCII files cannot be created or modified with the editor. These files include machine-level files (COM file type), HEX files created by the assembler, CBASIC intermediate language files (INT file type), and certain BASIC data files.

Here's the same information after you've arranged it in an easy-to-read list.

*Series in a List*

You cannot use the editor to create or modify files that are not ASCII files. These files include:

- Machine-level files (COM file type)
- HEX files created by the assembler
- CBASIC intermediate language files (INT file type)
- Certain BASIC data files

Don't go overboard in creating lists, however. Too many lists make your text seem choppy and disconnected. If you have three or four lists in a row, break them up with a solid paragraph.

The guidelines for writing lists are simple:

- Start your list with an introductory sentence.

- Use parallel grammatical structure.

- Be consistent with punctuation and capitalization.

- Limit the number of items. Eight items are the suggested maximum.

O  Use numbers or letters when list items are in chronological order or in order of importance, or when you need to refer to them in other parts of the document. Otherwise, bullets or dashes can be used.

INTRODUCING A LIST.   Begin a list with an introductory statement, as in the following example.

The following tools complete the inventory:

O  Three hacksaws
O  Four rasps
O  One hammer

MAKING LISTS CONSISTENT.   Be consistent when you write lists; use parallel grammatical structure and consistent punctuation for each list item. To see what happens to a list when you don't use parallel construction, take a look at the following:

*Inconsistent*

The Factory Insurance Association recommends the following safeguards on single-burner boiler furnaces:

O  A low-water cut-out switch.
O  An independent low-water fuel cut-off.
O  Excess pressure or limit cut-out switches shall be provided for steam boilers.
O  Spark-ignited interrupted-flame gas pilot shall be provided.

The first two items are consistent with each other because they're phrases that complete the sentence begun by the introduction. The last two items, however, are complete sentences in themselves. Here's the same list rewritten for consistency.

*Consistent*

The Factory Insurance Association recommends the following safeguards on single-burner boiler furnaces:

○ A low-water cut-out switch.

○ An independent low-water fuel cut-off.

○ An excess pressure or limit cut-out switch for steam boilers.

○ A spark-ignited interrupted-flame gas pilot.

Break up a series with more than eight items into two or more lists. For instance, you might have a list giving 24 possible reasons for deficiencies in hot-plant mix paving mixtures. After reviewing the list, you might find you can divide the items into three lists: one for faulty equipment operation, one for improper mixing procedures, and one for improper drying procedures.

Writing the modules that make up your documents is easy when you use the basic tools of composition described in this chapter. For more information about composition, check "Recommended Reference Books" at the end of this book. It lists some excellent resources on composition.

# Writing from Your Reader's Viewpoint

—Do you know which level of formality is suitable for your particular readers and your particular document?

—Do you know what degree of technicality meets your readers' needs?

—Do you show respect for your readers' intelligence?

—Do you tell readers why the information is relevant for them?

—Do you use a positive rather than a negative approach?

—Do you use unbiased and nonsexist language?

Have you ever read a document that seemed stilted or condescending? Or one that was written with technical jargon that only a handful of people in the whole world could possibly understand? You were, no doubt, either bored with the document or annoyed because the language did not reflect your attitude or your level of knowledge about the subject. To avoid this problem in *your* documents, choose language that your readers can both understand and identify with. This chapter describes how to establish a rapport with your readers by writing from their viewpoint.

## CHOOSING THE LEVEL OF FORMALITY

Should your writing style be personal and chatty? Or should it be reserved and authoritative? Or down-to-earth and straightforward? You use three varieties of English in your communications: informal, formal, and semiformal. Most of the time, for almost all technical documents, *semiformal English* (down-to-earth and straightforward) is the appropriate choice. On a rare occasion, if you had to write an official proclamation for an organization, for instance, or for a high-placed official, you might use *formal English* (reserved and dignified). *Informal English* (personal and chatty) is appropriate only for informal communications, such as a quick memo to a friend. Even in this circumstance, if the memo is going in the files, semiformal English is the better choice.

The following example shows two versions of a paragraph from an interoffice memo. The first one uses informal English and the second, formal English. Both are inappropriate.

*Informal English*

The floor panels have to hit the target date on the button. We all know what happens if they don't . . . a big 5% on the debit side.

*Formal English*

The Shipping Department must deliver the shipment of floor panels on or before June 6, 1986. If this crucial shipment is not delivered in a timely manner, a situation which must be avoided at all costs, Jones Manufacturing Company will have to recompense Brown, Ltd. a quite substantial sum, specifically a five percent penalty. Please notify your supervisor without delay of any potential problems that will affect this shipment.

Here's the same paragraph written in semiformal English. The style is straightforward, casual yet businesslike, appropriate to the readers' needs and the objectives of the memorandum.

*Semiformal English*

I want to remind you that we have to deliver the shipment of floor panels by June 11th. Otherwise, Brown, Ltd. will charge us a five percent penalty. Let me know if there will be any problems in meeting this deadline.

## WRITING SEMIFORMAL ENGLISH

How do you make your language semiformal? Here are some guidelines.

- O  Use small, plain words rather than long, fancy ones: *pay* rather than *recompense*, for instance.

- O  Use specific and concrete terms rather than general terms and abstractions: *memos* rather than *communications*, for instance.

- O  Use phrases from everyday speech like *look into* and *spell out*. Use *and, so*, and *that* instead of *furthermore, consequently*, and *wherein*.

- O  Use personal pronouns like *I* and *you*.

- O  Use contractions occasionally, such as *it's* or *you're*.

- O  Speak directly to the readers in a conversational tone. Even in those documents presenting educational material or instructions to a lay audience, use a tone that speaks to readers as equals in intelligence and status.

- O  Make requests of or suggestions to readers rather than issuing directives.

In the following example, an interoffice memo from one supervisor to another, note the straightforward casual tone, the use of personal pronouns and contractions, and the courteous request for support.

> Joan J. James, manager of avionics engineering at Smith Airlines, has written a report about her company's experiences with first-generation digital avionics. I think you and the other members of the Airlines Electronic Engineering Committee will find this report helpful in developing the new design guidelines. I'd appreciate it if you could ask one of your group to prepare an analysis of the report for discussion at the April 11th committee meeting.

## WRITING FORMAL ENGLISH

You may be assigned certain types of documents in which you think a more formal tone—one that's serious and dignified—would be appropriate. Generally, you might want to use formal English when:

- ○ The document is an official, policy-making report that will have wide distribution or a permanent place on bookshelves.

- ○ The document speaks officially for the organization or for a highly placed or highly respected person.

- ○ The readers of the document are highly placed or highly respected persons.

Even if you decide that your document needs formal English, use a light hand. Studies show that semiformal English is much more readable for all types of audiences, no matter their position or level of education. Here are some choices you can make in language, however, that will give your document a serious and dignified tone.

○ Use the official *we* rather than *I*.

○ Speak impersonally to your readers; don't address them directly as *you*.

○ Spell out words like *it is* or *you are* instead of using contractions.

○ Use moderately long sentences with more involved constructions along with shorter, simpler ones.

○ Issue directives to your readers instead of making requests of or suggestions to them.

In the following interoffice memo from a chief executive officer to his divisional vice presidents nationwide, note the lack of contractions. This executive maintained a dignified reserve by using *we* and by issuing a clear directive for action.

> Alexander Smith, manager of avionics engineering at CJC Avionics Inc., has written an excellent report on that company's experience with first-generation digital avionics. Smith concludes the report by proposing a number of rules for CJC's future avionics systems and equipment design. Please see that the directors in your division read the report and analyze the feasibility of incorporating these rules into the new design guidelines. We would like to have these studies in hand by November 30, 1986.

Remember, the occasions when you'll need to use formal English are few and far between. When in doubt, semiformal English is always the better choice.

## CHOOSING THE DEGREE OF TECHNICALITY

What degree of technicality should you use in the language of your document? Do you need to give the readers a lot of technical detail to accomplish the goals of the document? Do you have to explain technical concepts to them? Do you need to define most or all of the terms? Your document plan describes the readers' level of knowledge about both the field and the subject, and describes the goals of the document. This information is your guide to deciding what degree of technicality—high, moderate, or low—to use in your language.

Here are some general guidelines:

○ Define any terms that may be new to the readers.

○ Provide background material that will help readers understand the information, but only to the degree that it's necessary. If they don't need the details, leave them out.

○ Leave out theory, no matter how fascinating, if it doesn't help to accomplish the document's goals.

○ Keep any background material and explanations at the level that your readers need.

○ Give readers only the technical details necessary to accomplish the goals of the document.

○ Write for the readers with the lowest level of knowledge.

## WRITING FOR HIGHLY KNOWLEDGEABLE READERS

When you write for readers who are experts in the field, who need a high degree of technicality, you must consider the goals of your document. Generally, you run into two different situations.

1.  Your readers don't need many definitions, explanations, or background information to understand the document. You can assume that they have the technical background to understand the information you want to present.

2.  Your readers need to know, can understand, and can make use of myriad technical details that would be too complex for less expert readers.

In the following example, the information is for readers who are knowledgeable in the subject matter. The writer assumes that they're familiar with the terms and concepts mentioned and does not define the terms or provide background information.

> The new model uses a fly-by-wire control system, in which a computer sends signals to the hydraulic actuators powering the rudder, elevators, ailerons, and spoilers.

## WRITING FOR MODERATELY KNOWLEDGEABLE READERS

When you write for readers who have a background in the field and are generally knowledgeable about the subject, but who may not be experts, you need a moderate level of technicality in your language. Define terms, explain concepts, and provide enough background detail to meet their needs. For instance, managers who have only a broad overview of the functions of their departments would need more definition and explanation in a report than supervisors who are deeply involved in the day-to-day work.

For readers who require a medium level of technicality, we have a second version of the previous example. These readers are generally familiar with the subject, but probably need reminders about some of the details so that the information is more meaningful.

> The new model uses a fly-by-wire control system rather than traditional mechanical controls. A computer sends electronic signals to the hydraulic actuators (similar to control devices in a car's power steering), which control the rudder and the *elevators* (used to point the nose), the *ailerons* (used to roll when turning), and the *spoilers* (used to provide lift on takeoff and drag on landing).

## WRITING FOR UNKNOWLEDGEABLE READERS

When you write for readers who know very little about the field or the subject, you need to use language with a low level of technicality. Your approach depends on the information in your document plan. What do you want your readers to get from the document? How will they use it?

Give readers who need background material an overview, and present the technical material in the simplest form possible. Leave out theory, leave out details, and give the big picture, rather like the *Cliff Notes* summaries used in literature classes.

When these readers need technical details—to understand a subject or to learn how to do something, for instance—give them only the details they need. Present the technical information as clearly as possible, defining all terms and explaining all concepts necessary to accomplish your goals.

The final version of our example contains more definitions for readers who have only a lay knowledge of the subject.

> The new model uses a fly-by-wire control system rather than a mechanical control system. In this new system, a computer sends electronic signals to hydraulic *actuators* (pistonlike devices similar to those used in a car's power steering system). The hydraulic actuators move the *rudder* (which moves the plane's nose right or left), the *elevators* (which point the nose up or down), the *ailerons* (which roll the plane in a banked turn), and the *spoilers* (which add extra lift on takeoff and extra drag on landing).

## EXPLAINING RELEVANCE

Keep the needs of your readers in mind when you're dealing with an abundance of technical detail. When you begin a passage, tell them how or why the information is relevant. Give them a "for instance" example of how they might make use of the information or why they need to know it.

In passages containing lengthy technical detail, take your readers back to the concrete and specific every so often. Otherwise, they may lose sight of why the information is significant to them.

In the following example, the plunge into technical detail is too abrupt. Readers aren't told why they should know or care about these facts.

*Doesn't Explain Relevance*

> The utility program SMOUSE.EXE, a menu-making utility program, converts the mouse menu source program into an executable mouse menu file. All prewritten mouse menus include the source programs.

In this rewrite, an explanation of how the readers might want to use the information leads into the technical details.

*Explains Relevance*

You will probably want to use the mouse with other applications. You can do so by writing your own command menus. The Super Mouse package lets you write command menus in a programming language that is easy to understand. The utility program SMOUSE.EXE converts . . .

---

## RESPECTING YOUR READERS

---

Have you ever read a document written by an expert in a field other than your own and felt you were being patronized? Remember that feeling when you are called on to write a document for lay people in *your* field. Your language should reflect your respect for the readers' intelligence and their ability to understand your material. Never use simplistic language (such as you might use for children in grade school) or give over-elaborate explanations. The example below has a patronizing tone, because of the sequence of simple sentences, the repetition of the "preachy" word *duty*, and the admonishment, "be sure."

You have two main duties when you first come on shift. Your first duty is to check with the operator to see if anything has happened during the previous shift. Be sure to have a list of questions on hand so you'll not miss anything. Your second duty is to test the water-glass, column, valves, and piping.

The following version is straightforward and business-like and assumes that the reader has the intelligence to understand the procedure.

When you first come on shift:

1. Check with the operator to see if anything happened during the previous shift that needs your attention.
2. Test the water-glass, column, valves, and piping.

## USING A POSITIVE APPROACH

When you make recommendations and suggestions, use a positive approach rather than a negative or critical one. You're more likely to get a cooperative response and less likely to incur resentment. Here are examples of negative approaches followed by more appropriate positive approaches.

*Negative Approach*

If your department cannot deliver the plans on time, Palmer's design group will have to help you.

*Positive Approach*

Palmer's design group will be available if your department needs support in delivering the plans on time.

*Negative Approach*

Do not lay out the guide pins haphazardly.

*Positive Approach*

Lay out the guide pins in an orderly way.

## WRITING WITHOUT BIAS

Write with objective, unbiased language. When you interpret information, draw conclusions, and make recommendations, do so based on the facts. Even when you are trying
to persuade your readers to your point of view, you'll be
more effective using facts and logically drawn conclusions
than using emotionally colored language.

Here's an example of a sentence that contains biased
language. The quotation marks around *innovative* make the
word reek with sarcasm. That the technical achievement is
questionable is a conclusion better left unstated.

> Rogers, whose previous "innovative" efforts are well known, has
> once again staked his claim to fame on questionable technical
> achievements.

Here is the rewrite, minus the biased language.

> Rogers, whose QR-1 System was widely publicized last year,
> announced a new system at last month's meeting. Preliminary
> tests on the system, the QR-2, showed the following results...

Here's an example of another type of biased writing
from a marketing brochure. Notice the loaded words *special*
and *Maseratti engine*.

> If you're one of those special people who just have to push the
> speed limit, you'll appreciate this super-fast 80386 machine.
> SciTech Research knows that putting a Maseratti engine in a
> Volkswagen just gives you a fast Volkswagen. This machine's
> Maseratti performance was built from the ground up.

Most readers have become too sophisticated for this type
of manipulation, which appeals to their ego or desire for
status. The facts—details of the machine's performance,
comparisons with competing machines—would be much
more effective.

---

## CHOOSING NONSEXIST LANGUAGE

---

Many organizations, responding to the changing social climate, have published standards for acceptable nonsexist language. If your organization hasn't established such guidelines, you can adopt the ones below.

### CHOOSING GENERIC TITLES AND DESCRIPTIONS

Use titles and descriptions that are not explicitly male or female.

| Use | Rather than |
|---|---|
| supervisor, chief | foreman |
| service representative, technician | repairman |
| businessperson | businessman |
| chair or chairperson | chairman |
| representative | spokesman |
| worker | workman |
| assistant, key aide | right-hand man |
| flight attendant | stewardess |
| drafter | draftsman |
| big job | man-sized job |
| humans, humankind, people | mankind |

### CHOOSING NONSEXIST PRONOUNS AND ADJECTIVES

Your language should include all of your readers. Use pronouns that aren't exclusively male or female. Here are some simple techniques to avoid the he/she, his/her problem.

○  Use the plural form rather than the singular.

○  If the title has to be singular, substitute an article (a, an, the) for a pronoun.

○  Address the readers directly, if possible.

Here are some examples:

*Nonsexist: Plural Form*

Supervisors should route their checklists to everyone on their list.

All operators must find ways to deal with disruptions.

*Nonsexist: Singular Form*

The supervisor should route the checklist to everyone on the list.

Each operator must find ways to deal with disruptions.

*Nonsexist: Direct Address*

You should route the checklist to everyone on the list.

You must find ways to deal with disruptions.

*Sexist*

The supervisor should route the checklist to everyone on his list.

Each operator must find her own way to deal with disruptions.

Referring to the document plan, with its profile of the readers and definition of the document's goals, will help you decide what level of formality and degree of technicality to use. Showing the relevance of information, respecting your readers, using a positive approach, writing without bias, and using nonsexist language are all techniques that will help you write from your readers' viewpoint.

# CHAPTER 11

# Using Lean, Clear, and Strong Language

USING PLAIN LANGUAGE

CHOOSING SPECIFIC AND CONCRETE
WORDS

WRITING WITH ACTIVE VERBS

USING THE PROPER TENSE

—Do you choose words that are short and plain?

—Do you use language that is concise and to the point?

—Do you choose words that are specific and concrete?

—Do you use active verbs most of the time?

—Do you use the appropriate tense?

These days, politicians, bureaucrats, and yes, even some writers, place great value on "one-liners," euphemisms, and on trendy words and phrases invented to suit their purposes. Grandiose language may sound impressive at first but, because content is missing, people are often left shaking their heads in puzzlement.

If you want your document to achieve your goals, use language that is plain, concise, specific, and direct. Simplicity and clarity are especially important in technical writing. Fancy, wordy, abstract, weak, and vague language can easily blunt the impact of a document and obscure its meaning.

This chapter describes how to use plain language, specific and concrete words, active verbs, and the proper tense to give clarity and vigor to your writing.

## USING PLAIN LANGUAGE

You'll always reach readers with plain language, even in formal writing. Not only is plain language easier to remember than fancy language, it's easier to understand as well. A plain word is better than a fancy one, a short and simple sentence is better than a long, convoluted one, and a one- or two-syllable word is generally better than a three- or four-syllable one.

You can irritate readers with elaborate language and euphemisms and lead them to discount what you have to say. By choosing simple, plain language, and being concise, you can write documents that are clear and effective.

### CHOOSING SIMPLE WORDS

If you have to choose between a short simple word and a long fancy one, choose the simple one. Your meaning will be much clearer. To see what we're talking about, take a look at the example below. Not only is the language pompous, but the meaning is fuzzy too.

> In making preparations, ascertain that you will have an assistant available to maintain a grip on a tool of illumination at one end of each tube while you conduct your examination of the tube from the other end.

Exaggerated? Maybe. But, we all tend to use elaborate language to some degree. Here's the same paragraph written with plain words. See how much clearer it is.

> Before you begin, make sure you have a helper on hand who can hold a light at one end of the tube while you look in the other end.

The rewrite is not only easier to understand, it also frees up space you can use for other vital information.

Here's a list of short and simple words to use instead of their fancy counterparts.

| USE | INSTEAD OF |
| --- | --- |
| now | at this point in time |
| say, write, tell | communicate |
| do | implement |
| show, point out | indicate |
| help, assist | facilitate |
| try | attempt |
| find out, discover, correct, set, learn | ascertain |
| buy | procure |
| permit, call for | warrant |
| by, following, per, under | pursuant to |
| rank | prioritize |
| method | methodology |
| best, most, greatest | optimum |
| meet, work with | interface with |
| end | expiration |
| speed up, hasten | expedite |
| fair | equitable |
| give, issue, pass | disseminate |
| many | appreciable |
| near | close proximity |
| is, makes up | constitutes |

This list is just a sampling, of course. You can probably think of many more examples.

## BEING CONCISE

You can give your writing more clarity and strength by writing short and simple sentences and by avoiding wordiness.

### WRITING SHORT, SIMPLE SENTENCES.

Short, simple sentences are easier to understand than long, involved ones. However, a string of short sentences can be monotonous. You want to vary the lengths of your sentences, mixing in a few longer, slightly more involved ones with your short ones.

The following example shows how a long, run-on sentence that contains many modifying phrases ends up obscuring the meaning of the sentence.

> The ring is bound to wear in time, of course, and without the advantage of adjustment, leakage around the plunger will slowly increase, finally becoming so great that a new ring will be required, involving considerable replacement expense.

In the version below, we have broken the information into two short sentences and one moderately long one.

> The ring is bound to wear in time, of course. Without adjustment, leakage around the plunger will slowly increase and finally become so great that a new ring will be required. The replacement expense will be considerable.

AVOIDING WORDINESS.    If you want clean, clear language, watch out for:

○ Noun clusters (*structured learning environment* instead of *classroom*)

○ Prepositional phrases (*as a result of* instead of *because*)

○ Redundancies (*repeat again* instead of *repeat*)

○ Unnecessary words (*really and truly* instead of *truly*)

The following example shows how noun clusters, prepositional phrases, redundancies, and unnecessary words can clutter your writing.

> As a result of our conversations with the investigators, our suspicions were confirmed. We are of the definite opinion that one of the profit-leveling factors this year is the involuntary conversion of assets.

Translation? In the following revision, we've removed the noun clusters, the prepositional phrases, the redundancy, and the wordiness to reveal the meaning.

> The investigators confirmed our suspicions that theft is the reason for lower profits this year.

Here are examples of plain words you can use instead of some typical noun clusters.

| USE | INSTEAD OF |
|---|---|
| problems | design constraint considerations |
| mistake | quality reduction factor |
| good, excellent | state of the art |

These plain words are good substitutes for some common prepositional phrases.

| USE | INSTEAD OF |
|---|---|
| about | of the order of magnitude |
| more | in excess of |
| for | in the amount of |
| because | as a result of |
| know | aware of the fact that |
| now | at this point in time |
| to | in order to |
| must | it is essential that |
| for | for the purpose of |
| about, regarding | in reference to |

These words can replace redundancies.

| USE | INSTEAD OF |
|---|---|
| current, existing | currently existing |
| eliminate, end | eliminate completely |
| spell out, explain | spell out in detail |
| small | small in size |
| yellow | yellow in color |
| essential, necessary | absolutely essential |
| different | various different |
| conclusion, end | final conclusion |
| introduce | first introduced |
| without | totally devoid of |
| entering | first entering |

| | |
|---|---|
| straight, linear | straight linear |
| consensus | general consensus |
| innovation | new innovation |
| near | close proximity |
| oval | oval in shape |
| right, proper | right and proper |
| halves | two equal halves |
| reason | reason why |
| cooperation | mutual cooperation |
| result | end result |
| continue | continue on |

Here is a list of plain words you can use in place of some common wordy phrases.

| USE | INSTEAD OF |
|---|---|
| because | due to the fact that |
| most | the majority of |
| could | would be able to |
| obvious | readily apparent |
| indicate, show | be an indication of |
| remind you | call your attention to the fact that |
| allow | afford an opportunity |

These lists contain only a few examples to remind you to look for noun clusters, prepositional phrases, redundancies, and just plain wordiness. You'll run into many more examples—we are all guilty of wordiness—so be alert and watch out for them in your writing.

## CHOOSING SPECIFIC AND CONCRETE WORDS

Specific, concrete words add clarity and energy to your writing. Let's look at the following example. The first sentence is vague, while the revised version, because it is specific, is meaningful.

*General*

The inspectors rejected many parts.

*Specific*

The inspectors rejected ten percent (20 out of 200) of the floor panels.

Here's another example. The first sentence is vague. The second one is not only specific, it uses concrete words that add color and energy.

*General*

We found the cutting room was not well maintained.

*Specific*

In the cutting room, the floor was littered with shavings and debris, the tools encrusted with grease and grime.

The second description of the floor and the tools make a vivid picture for the readers.

---
## WRITING WITH ACTIVE VERBS
---

Use active verbs in most of your sentences to make your writing forceful and direct. Passive verbs weaken your language and make it seem vague and lacking in authority. (We describe some exceptions to this general rule later on in this section.)

Here are some examples of active verbs and passive verbs.

*Active*

The operator *signs* the sheet.

*Passive*

The sheet must *be signed.*

*Active*

Water *floods* the chamber.

*Passive*

The chamber *is flooded* with water.

When you read your drafts, look for words like *is, was, are, be, is being, are being,* and *have been* in your sentences. Try to replace them with active verbs to make the sentence more direct and energetic.

Using active verbs benefits your writing in another way: when you use an active verb, you must name the *agent* (the person or thing that takes the action). In the example below, for instance, who is supposed to close and lock the valves? The readers have no way of knowing.

*Passive*

All valves, particularly the blow down and the main stop, should be closed and locked in the closed position.

When we rewrite the sentence with an active verb, it not only has more vitality, it becomes specific. We name the agent (the engineer) who takes the action (closing and locking the valves).

*Active*

The engineer should close all valves, particularly the blow down and the main stop, and lock them in the closed position.

Here's another example that shows how a passive verb weakens the message.

*Passive*

Before etching, a *resist* material is put on top of the copper foil to protect it. Once the electronic circuit has been designed, it is copied onto the copper foil in one of several ways.

See how much more alive and direct the following revision sounds.

*Active*

Before you begin etching, put a *resist* material on top of the copper foil to protect it. After you finish designing the electronic circuit, you can copy it onto the copper foil in one of several ways.

In a few cases, however, you'll want to use a passive verb: when the agent is unknown or when you need to be indirect and impersonal to avoid offending someone. Here are examples of the passive voice in sentences where the agents are unknown.

*Acceptable Passive Verb*

The success of the venture was well publicized.

The panel had obviously been badly used.

In the next example, the use of the active verb makes the sentence too blunt.

*Unacceptable Active Verb*

Your department has to revise the faulty configuration management procedure by June 3rd.

The following version sounds less accusing and will probably gain more cooperation and certainly more good will.

*Acceptable Passive Verb*

Our configuration management procedures need to be revised. Can your department draft a proposal by June 3rd?

## USING THE PROPER TENSE

Which tense should you write in: past, present, or future? Here are a few guidelines to help you choose.

○ Use the present tense to give instructions or to give information, general truths, hypotheses, principles, and theories.

○ Use the past tense to report or document the results of studies, experiments, and research and to narrate historical background.

○ Use the future tense sparingly, when you are actually speaking of what is going to or what could happen.

## USING THE PRESENT TENSE

When you write instructions or explain theories, the present tense gives a sense of immediacy that the past and future tenses cannot. Most of us have to curb the tendency, at least once in awhile, to write in the future tense.

In the following example, the use of the future tense weakens the instruction.

> If you are going to write a program, your first step will be to type the command NEW. This command will erase any program already in memory.

When we rewrite the instruction in the present tense, the instruction is definite, firm. The sentence tells the readers to type the command, not at some indefinite date in the future, but now and whenever they want to write a program.

> To write a program, first type the command NEW. This command erases any program already in memory.

## USING THE PAST TENSE

Use the past tense to describe what has happened, to describe the results of studies, and to narrate histories. For instance, you might need to give readers the history of a process—explaining how and why it came into use—before you explain its specific application for your organization. You'd use the past tense to narrate the history of the process and the present tense to describe the application.

The following paragraph is an example of how you might use the past tense to describe what has happened.

> In the early 1970s, Europe realized that there would be a commercial future for space transportation in the 1980s. At that time, there was some question as to whether the Space Shuttle would ever get off the ground.

## USING THE FUTURE TENSE

Use the future tense occasionally, only when it's appropriate and natural to do so, when you're actually speaking of what's going to or what could happen. Using the future tense when it's not appropriate, however, makes your writing sound hesitant and lacking in authority.

Here's an example of the proper use of the future tense.

When you start the machine using the procedure described above, you will not have any problems.

When you're writing and revising, keep a close watch on the language you use. Plain and simple language, conciseness, active verbs, and the proper tense make your writing clear, direct, and forceful. If you would like to read more about using the English language, see "Recommended Reference Books" at the end of this book.

# Writing Instructions and Persuasive Passages

WRITING INSTRUCTIONS

CHOOSING PERSUASIVE STRATEGIES

—Are your instructions organized and complete?

—Do you support your instructions with illustrations and examples?

—Do you plan your tactics before you write persuasive material?

—Do you use a logical order to organize persuasive material?

You'll often be called on to write both instructions and persuasive material. This chapter describes how to write instructions that are clear and easy to follow and persuasive passages that will win your case.

## WRITING INSTRUCTIONS

Readers appreciate clear and easy-to-follow instructions that help them do their work efficiently. The general guidelines for writing instructions are:

O  Write complete instructions; include every step, tell readers what will happen as well as what to do.

○ Organize instructions into lists of numbered steps.

○ Use parallel grammatical structure.

○ Limit the number of steps in your instructions to eight.

○ Use illustrations to support your text.

○ Use examples to make the instructions clearer.

## WRITING COMPLETE INSTRUCTIONS

Follow these guidelines to make your instructions as complete as possible:

○ If you can, watch someone do the task or do it yourself before you begin to write. Note every step, every result.

○ Assume nothing. Write down every step in the procedure.

○ Describe what happens as well as the actions to take. Describe the results of each action, what a machine does, for instance, *after* the reader performs the step. Describe anything that might possibly confuse readers so they won't be frustrated by uncertainty.

○ Test your instructions after you've written them. Do the task yourself if at all possible or find someone who can do the task and ask that person to test the instructions.

## ORGANIZING INSTRUCTIONS INTO NUMBERED STEPS

Always organize instructions into numbered steps rather than burying them in long paragraphs. Numbered steps are most effective because they help readers keep their place while they follow the instructions and find the instructions again when they refer to them after the initial reading.

Numbered steps also add white space and variety to the printed page, making the document less intimidating and more visually appealing.

The process of writing instructions step by step also helps you to be precise and thorough.

Here's an example of how *not* to write instructions.

### Buried Instructions

To select a format for your page numbers, first choose the Page Layout command from the Format menu. Choose "Automatic Page Numbers" and then select one of the options in "Page Number Format." To carry out the command, press the ENTER key.

Here's the same set of instructions arranged in a numbered, step-by-step list.

### Instructions in a Numbered List

To select a format for your page numbers:

1. Choose the Page Layout command from the Format Menu.
2. Choose "Automatic Page Numbers."
3. Select one of the options in "Page Number Format."
4. Press the ENTER key to carry out the command.

The second version is much easier to follow, isn't it?

## USING PARALLEL GRAMMATICAL STRUCTURE

Just as you should use parallel grammatical structure in lists, you should also use it in instructions. Commands, words such as *choose, wash, press, switch,* are most effective because they are direct and authoritative.

To illustrate the difference, look at the following example which shows a set of instructions written with a grammatical structure that's not parallel.

*Unparallel Grammatical Structure*

To mount the circuit board:

1. Two additional holes should be drilled in the opposite end of the board for mounting screws.
2. Use plastic spacers to hold the board assembly in place.
3. Twist the interconnecting wires between the board and the panel components into a cable.
4. The front and rear panel components should be mounted.

Here's the same set of instructions rewritten with parallel grammatical structure. Each step is a command beginning with an active verb.

*Parallel Grammatical Structure*

To mount the circuit board:

1. Drill two additional holes in the opposite end of the board for mounting screws.
2. Use plastic spacers to hold the board assembly in place.
3. Twist the interconnecting wires between the board and the panel components into a cable.
4. Mount the front and rear panel components.

## LIMITING THE NUMBER OF STEPS

Whenever possible, you should have no more than eight steps in any set of instructions. When a procedure has more than eight steps, try to break it down into two or more logical segments. For instance, 24 steps describing how to change the paper in a printer could be broken into three sets of instructions, one explaining how to remove the paper cartridge, one explaining how to load the new paper, and one explaining how to check that the paper is loaded properly.

## USING ILLUSTRATIONS

An illustration or a photograph can make a procedure clear in a way that words alone cannot. For instance, if you tell a reader to push the red switch located on the side of the machine, an illustration that shows the exact location of the switch saves the reader time and uncertainty.

Guidelines for using illustrations in a set of instructions are:

- ○ Keep the illustration simple and uncluttered.
- ○ Position the illustration as close as possible to the text it supports.
- ○ Tell the reader where the illustration is located when you have to position it at a distance from the text it supports. (For example, write "See Figure 9.3 on the following page.")

Here's a set of instructions followed by an illustration that shows readers exactly what to do.

*Instructions with Illustration*

To select the temperature for heating:

1. Set the left lever to the energy savings temperature you want when the building is unoccupied.

2. Set the right lever to the temperature you want for normal comfort during working hours.

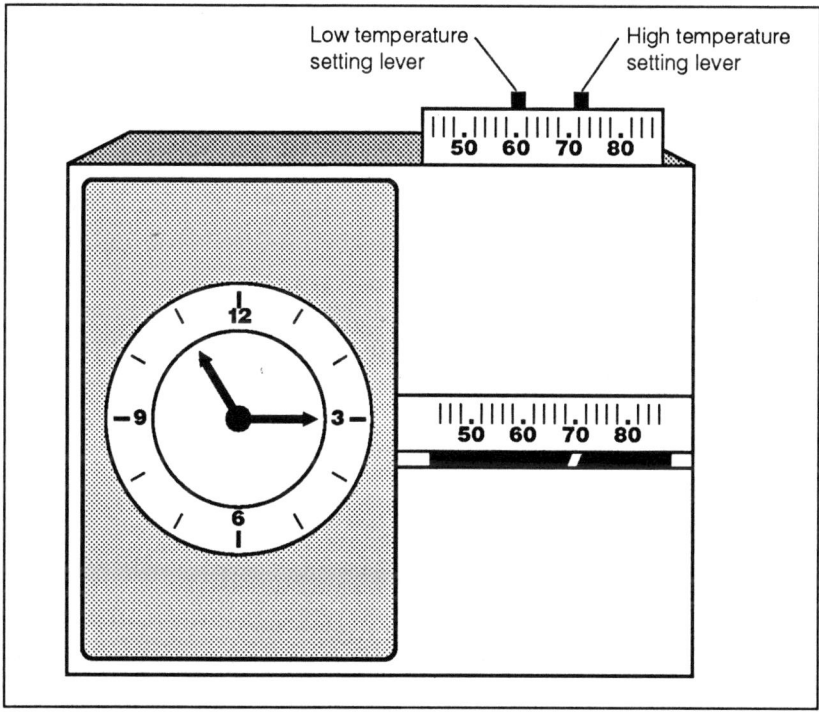

**Figure 1.1.** Temperature Settings.

## USING EXAMPLES

Examples clarify technical information. Use them whenever possible to make your instructions easier for readers to follow.

The guidelines for writing examples are:

○ Choose examples appropriate to your readers' level of knowledge.

○ Keep examples brief.

○ Choose examples that are as interesting as possible, easy to say but not always easy to do.

To choose an appropriate example, make use of the information in your document plan. How will the readers use the information in your document? How much do they know about the field? The subject matter? What examples would they find both practical and interesting?

For instance, if you were teaching readers new to the BASIC programming language how to write a LET statement, you could support your text with the example that follows.

*(Text)*

Use the LET statement to assign a value to a *variable*. Variables are "names" given to numbers or to phrases that contain both numbers as well as letters and certain other characters. In this section, we'll consider only "numeric" variables, those that give names to numbers.

To write a LET statement, type LET, followed by the variable, an equal sign, and the numeric value assigned to the variable.

*(Example)*

Here are examples of LET statements:

>       LET A = 5
>       LET A2 = 8
>       LET ALPHA = 10

Always use an example when the instructions are hard to explain. When a sentence or two is not enough to clarify a step in a set of instructions, you probably need to give the readers an example. In the following instructions, an example helps clarify the first step in a complex procedure.

*(Text)*

To estimate the water system capacity:

1. Estimate the amount of water used by animals. For example, suppose a farm has 50 milking cows, 30 dry cows, and 400 chickens. Your calculations might look like this:

*(Example)*

>       50 milking cows @ 35 gallons/cow = 1750 gal.
>       30 dry cows @ 15 gallons/cow       = 450 gal.
>       400 chickens @ 6 gallons/100       = 24 gal.
>             Total Daily Usage                2224 gal.

## CHOOSING PERSUASIVE STRATEGIES

You may need to write a claim letter that convinces others to repair a piece of equipment or refund your money, or a memo that convinces department heads that they should change procedures. Or you might write a report that convinces an organization that your company can do a better job for them than competing companies. In each of these cases, your document must persuade others to take action or to change their point of view.

## PLANNING YOUR APPROACH

Before you can persuade your readers, you need to persuade yourself. Here are steps to take to prepare yourself to write persuasive passages.

- O Think the problem through.
- O Assume that your readers disagree with your point of view and that they will find every possible flaw in your argument.
- O Write down the points you need to make to win the readers' agreement.
- O Identify existing points of agreement.
- O Lay out the evidence both for and against your point of view.
- O Decide on the logical arguments.

Now that you know the pros of your case as well as the cons, you're ready to lead your readers through this same process. Here are some guidelines for presenting your case:

- O Present the points of agreement to your readers.
- O Present the possible arguments against your point of view and then refute them.
- O Present your evidence exactly and fully. Stick to the facts.

## ORGANIZING PERSUASIVE PASSAGES

To make your argument persuasive, you'll use one or more of the logical orders discussed in Chapter 5, "Basics of Outlining." We discuss the most commonly used ones here: problem-cause-solution, cause-to-effect, and comparison-and-contrast. Other logical orders useful in persuasive writing are: effect-to-cause order, order of descending importance, order of utility, general-to-specific order, and acceptable-to-unacceptable order.

USING THE PROBLEM-CAUSE-SOLUTION ORDER. In the following example, the goal of the document is to persuade a supervisor to change departmental procedures. The supervisor has high-level knowledge of the operation, so the writer can assume that the technical details will be understood.

| | |
|---|---|
| *Problem* | The on-site test in April produced many spurious track initiations. In one instance, a single satellite alone had six track initiations. |
| *Cause* | Erroneous chirp-slope caused this problem. The chirp-slope pre-distortion cannot be correct when the track pulses for two objects on two separate faces are transmitted simultaneously. When the chirp-slope is erroneous, it results in pulse splitting; a single satellite produces a radar echo which, after pulse compression, gives two or three distinct returns. |
| *Solution* | I suggest we change our procedure by not transmitting two track pulses on two faces simultaneously. The chirp-slope will then be correct. |

USING THE CAUSE-TO-EFFECT ORDER. This example shows how to use the cause-to-effect order. The goal of the document is to persuade the purchasing agent (who has low-level technical knowledge) to purchase a different type of oil. The writer first explains what happens in the air compressor system (the causes) and then ends dramatically with the effect.

Cause    When the operators use a viscous oil in an air cylinder rather than a more fluid one, a greater quantity of oil collects. The oil mixes with dirt and forms into a hard deposit, made mostly of carbon, which clogs piston rings and valves. A quantity of these deposits, plus moisture and heat, produces gas, principally CO, which ignites at 1204°. When a leaky discharge valve allows compressed and heated air to reenter the machine, the air is recompressed and further heated. In time, the temperature is high enough to ignite the CO.

Effect    An explosion is the result.

USING THE COMPARE-AND-CONTRAST ORDER.   When you want to convince someone that your method or your product is superior to other methods or products, the compare-and-contrast order is effective.

In the following example, the document's goal is to convince a customer that the Tagalong laptop computer is the best one available.

The Tagalong and the Mitey-Mite laptops are equal in RAM, clock speed, and the number of ports they offer. The Tagalong is superior in these important ways:

| TAGALONG | MITEY-MITE |
|---|---|
| 88-key standard | 76-key nonstandard |
| Two 720K floppy drives | Two 360K floppy drives |
| Math Coprocessor socket | No Math Coprocessor socket |

The details are listed in order of descending importance, putting the item that will most impress the prospective customer first.

USING OTHER LOGICAL ORDERS.   In some persuasive writing, you must give your readers background information before presenting your argument (the order of utility). For instance, if you recommend that your organization purchase a certain manufacturer's computer-aided-design equipment, you'll probably compare its performance with that of other available equipment. Your readers might first need some information on just what constitutes superior performance for this type of computer-aided-design equipment before they can weigh your evidence.

In other persuasive passages, you may have to present a large number of facts that could seem overwhelming and confusing to the readers. You can often use the general-to-specific order to group the information into categories that make it easier for readers to grasp. For instance, if you want to persuade people in your field to accept a new technology, you might group your arguments about its potential into topics like: increased profit, safer working conditions, growth, flexibility.

In other instances, when you know that readers will have certain objections to your recommendation or proposal, you can make good use of the acceptable-to-unacceptable order. Give readers information that is attractive or agreeable first, get them on your side, and then they will be in a better frame of mind to accept the other, less attractive points. For example, if you're proposing a change in office procedures that will mean initial expense for the company because of retraining for personnel, purchases of new equipment, and so on, tell the readers first about the long-term savings and the increase in productivity.

# CHAPTER 13

# Defining, Describing, and Explaining

DEFINING TERMS AND CONCEPTS

DESCRIBING AND EXPLAINING

—Are your definitions clear and exact?

—Are your descriptions concrete and vivid?

—Do you use logical orders to organize your descriptions and explanations?

—Do you use illustrations and examples to help readers understand your descriptions and explanations?

In technical writing, you must often define terms, describe objects and processes, and explain concepts. This chapter gives guidelines to help you define, describe, and explain clearly, vividly, and effectively.

## DEFINING TERMS AND CONCEPTS

A definition is a brief, careful explanation of the meaning of a term. When we define a term, we can do it with a statement, with qualifying phrases, or even with a single synonym. Often we expand a definition by restating it or by adding details and examples. Here are some guidelines for writing definitions:

○ Define each new term the first time you mention it in your document.

○ When your document is long, define each new term the first time you mention it at the beginning of each section or chapter.

○ Define the term immediately after you mention it.

○ Add visual emphasis to the term, its definition, or both by italicizing, underlining, or putting quotation marks around the term, or by putting parentheses around the definition.

○ Provide the amount of detail in the definition necessary to achieve your goals or to meet the readers' needs.

○ Describe what makes the term different when it is one of a group of similar things.

○ Provide examples, illustrations, or both, when the concept is difficult to pin down.

Here are examples of some simple definitions:

*Sample Definitions*

The primary flight controls include the *control yoke* (a steering-wheel-like control on most planes, a control stick on others), the rudder pedals, and the throttle.

Once you have formulated the problem and precisely defined all elements, you must then take the mathematical step of *optimization* (searching for the best decision).

The pump delivers the water from the well or other water source to a tank where it is held under pressure. (The term *pump* normally refers to both the pump itself and a motor, usually electric, which together make up the pumping unit.)

Here's an example of a definition that needs an illustration to make it clearer.

*Definition with Illustration*

A drain trap uses a chamber arranged to hold liquids. The trap prevents air from escaping from pipes, while allowing the flow of liquids. Figure 1.1 shows a typical drain trap design.

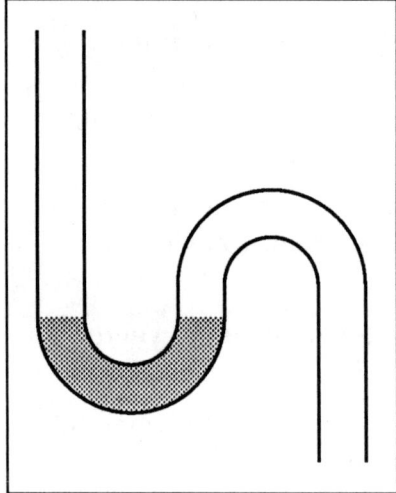

**Figure 1.1.** Drain Trap.

The following definition requires more detail and amplification.

*Definition*

Another problem is external corrosion of the boiler caused by leaks, erosion, embrittlement of the boiler plate, and *bagging*. Bagging is a bulge on the boiler plate formed when an accumulation of scale, oil, or dirt collects on the plate and comes between it and the water. The plate overheats, becomes soft and pliable, and is no longer able to withstand the pressure within the boiler. The pressure pushes the boiler plate out, creating a bulge, or bag.

The writer might have defined a *bag* as a bulge on the boiler plate, but in the context of the document, the readers need to know how a bag is formed. The definition in this case includes a description of a process.

The following example defines a concept that is hard to explain with words alone. The illustration helps it along.

*Definition of a Concept*

Specify the paper orientation that you want. If you want the picture to print vertically (sideways), choose **Landscape**. If you want the picture to print horizontally (the way it appears on the screen), choose **Portrait**. Figure 2.1 illustrates each option.

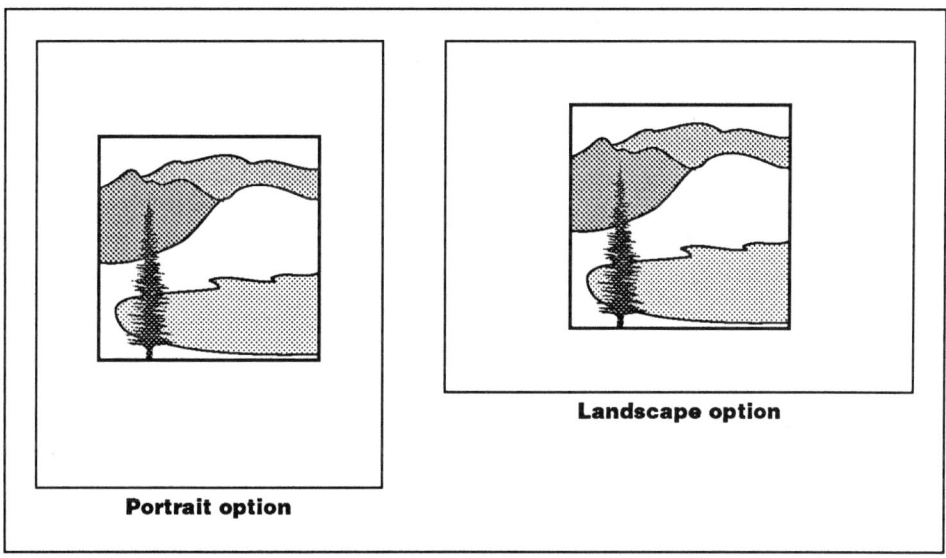

Portrait option

Landscape option

**Figure 2.1.** Paper Orientation Options.

## DESCRIBING AND EXPLAINING

When you write a description or an explanation, you answer some (occasionally all) of those time-honored questions of good reporting: Who? What? When? Where? How? Why?

What is it?

Who uses it?

When do they use it?

What happened?

When does (or did) it happen?

Where is it?

Where did it happen?

What does it do?

What is it made of?

What does it look like?

How is it put together?

How is it used?

How does it work?

The guidelines for writing clear, vivid descriptions and lucid explanations are:

○  Use a limiting title.

○  Give the big picture first (the general-to-specific order).

○  Use concrete, exact words.

○  Use illustrations and examples when they will help.

## USING A LIMITING TITLE

Introduce the description or the explanation with a title or a statement that tells the readers precisely what the subject is. What they expect should be what they get. If you're going to describe only the computer's display screen, announce your description as "The Display Screen," not "The Appearance of the XYZ Computer."

## GIVING THE BIG PICTURE FIRST

Use the general-to-specific order to give readers an overview before you get into the details. For a complex topic, organize the material by breaking it up into its major parts. For instance, if you're describing the behavior of Balaenidae whales, you might first give an overview of whale behavior and then proceed to describe the behavior of the four species of Balaenidae whales: northern right, southern right, pygmy right, and bowhead whales.

## USING PRECISE AND CONCRETE DETAIL

For descriptions and explanations that are clear and effective, you must record facts and details accurately and concretely. What do you and the readers see, hear, feel, or smell? Use precise and concrete language to bring the facts to life. A partition that is "nine feet, six inches high" sounds more impressive than one that is "tall." Readers can see an axe that is "rusty, with a dull cutting edge" and they'll remember the image. They won't remember an axe that is "in poor condition."

## USING ILLUSTRATIONS

Illustrations—drawings, diagrams, and photographs—help the text get the picture across to the readers. Use as many of them as possible. Chapter 4, "Planning Illustrations and Document Design," gives an overview of the many types of illustrations you can use.

## ARRANGING DETAILS IN LOGICAL ORDER

When you describe unmoving objects, use spatial order. When you describe processes or events, use chronological order. When you give readers background information so that they can understand specific details, use the order of utility. When you have several parts to describe, use the general-to-specific order.

In a complex explanation, you might use a combination of two or more of these logical orders. For instance, in explaining an automatic water system, you might give the readers the big picture first (order of utility), listing the parts of the water system in chronological order according to the flow of the water:

1. The tank or water source.

2. The pumping system.

3. The connections.

4. The distribution or piping system.

5. The control valves.

6. The switches.

Then you could use the spatial order to describe the appearance and location of the parts. Finally, you could use chronological order again to describe how each part of the system works.

## DESCRIBING A PROCESS

You use chronological order to describe a process, to tell readers what happens, what is going to happen, what could happen, or what has happened. How was the panel first cut, then trimmed, bored, and drilled? What happened in the experiment? In this example, the writer describes the first part of a process: determining the shape of an asteroid.

> The astronomer, located within the shadow of the asteroid (cast onto the Earth by the star), can see the asteroid approaching the star for several nights. Shortly before occulting the star, the asteroid image will merge with the star image. Then the star will suddenly blink out as the shadow of the asteroid crosses the observing astronomer. A few seconds, or a minute or two later, the star will blink on again. By timing the exact moments of blink-off and blink-on, the astronomer can calculate the size of the shadow.

## DESCRIBING OBJECTS

Use the spatial order to describe motionless objects such as buildings, machines, photographs, or illustrations.

In the following example, the writer uses the spatial order and supports the description with an illustration. The description of the stick, which foresters use to measure large trees, is detailed, concrete, and exact. The spatial order begins at the top and moves to the bottom. Note how the overview in the first sentence starts readers off with a basic image of the object.

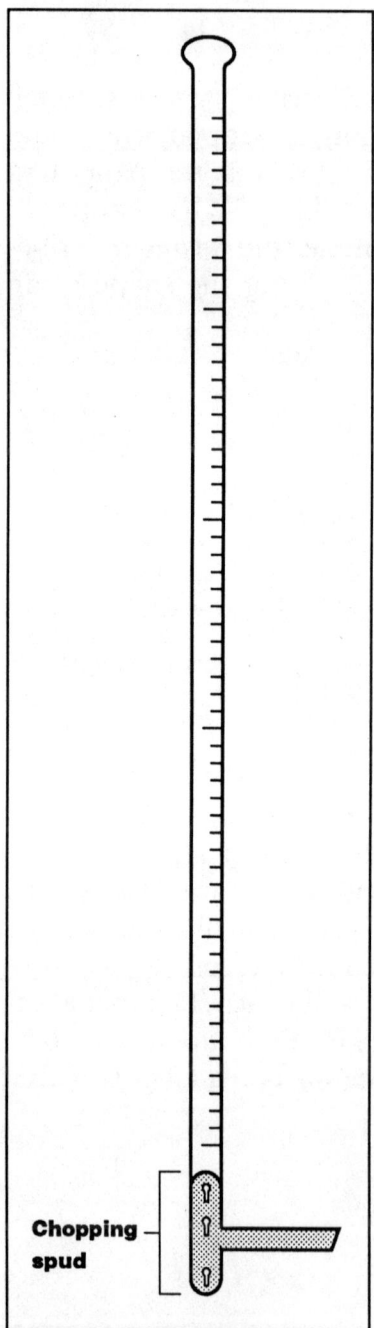

**Figure 1.1.** Columbia River
Water Stick.

THE COLUMBIA RIVER WATER STICK

The Columbia River water stick, used by scalers to measure a tree's diameter, is a long, thin wooden stick over six feet long. It has a long wooden handle, tipped with an iron chopping spud that has a metal prong welded to the spud at right angles to the handle. The handle is graduated from 0 to 72 inches or less, depending on the length of the stick. The chopping spud extends 7 inches beyond the prong and tapers to a sharp, broad point which is used for cutting into the log to test for defects. The prong, also 7 inches long, is attached with the upper edge exactly at the zero graduation. The scaler uses the prong to hold the stick in position for an accurate measurement of the diameter.

## DESCRIBING A COMPLEX MECHANISM

When you describe a complex mechanism you combine descriptions of objects and processes. Using the techniques of classification, partition, and subordination, the description can be broken up into three modules, as follows:

| | |
|---|---|
| General description | Describe the mechanism and what it does in general terms. Define the principle of operation (if necessary) and list the parts. |
| Description of parts | Define the part; describe its shape, dimensions, material; explain its function and how it relates to other parts. |
| Description of operation | Describe how the parts interrelate and then go through one complete operating cycle. |

## EXPLAINING COMPLEX CONCEPTS

Many concepts need more than a brief explanation. In the following example, the writer introduces an idea that's hard to explain to a lay audience. The explanation includes a definition and an example that help make the concept clearer.

> Catastrophe theory belongs to the branch of mathematics known as topology, a field (like geometry) that deals with phenomena numerically and visually. According to catastrophe theory, discontinuous events can be represented by certain geometrical shapes. For example, a topologist interested in forecasting the behavior of the stock market would not only use statistical analysis, but would also express such important economic variables as "speculation" and "demand" as factors in constant motion on a geometrical surface. A market crash is represented by a sudden drop from one surface to a lower one.

# PART FOUR

# REVIEWS, REVISIONS, AND FINAL DRAFTS

# CHAPTER 14

# Conducting
# a Review

PREPARING FOR A REVIEW

HANDLING REVIEW COMMENTS

—Do you give the people reviewing your document specific instructions?

—Do you have a method for handling reviewers' comments and corrections?

Every writer, no matter how experienced, can benefit from the help of others. Having experts, colleagues, or editors review your document is especially important in technical writing where clarity and precision are essential. Reviewers can point out areas that need clarification, information that you've left out, and mistakes.

How many reviews you go through depends on the type of document you're writing. A long document with significant impact may require two or more reviews; a simple document may need only one.

Whatever the length or type of document, a well-prepared review will improve it.

## PREPARING FOR A REVIEW

How much a review can help your document depends on how well you prepare for it. Although it's nice to hear "Looks good to me. Send it out," this type of comment doesn't improve the document. The guidelines for preparing for a helpful review are:

○ Schedule the review at the right time.

○ Give your reviewers a reminder a few days before you send out the review copies.

○ Make sure you prepare the draft of your document adequately.

○ Write a cover sheet for the review copies that gives specific instructions to the reviewers.

### MAKING YOUR REVIEW TIMELY

Be sure your reviews are timely, neither too early nor too late. If your document is still full of blank segments, it's not ready for a review. A few areas of missing information are fine, but reviewers must have enough material to respond to, even though you suspect some of the information may be incomplete or incorrect. If you have chosen your reviewers well and told them exactly what you want from them, they will supply the correct information.

If about 90 percent of the time allotted on your schedule for completing the document has already passed, it's too late for a review. Your reviewers won't have enough time to do a thorough job and you won't have enough time to make corrections.

For a long document, you might want to divide it into sections and review each section as it's completed. This is one way to give both you and your reviewers time to do a good job.

## NOTIFYING REVIEWERS IN ADVANCE

When you created your document plan, you included a list of reviewers. Your reviewers may include technical experts, editors, proofreaders, your supervisor, and marketing people. For instance, depending on your needs, you might have one reviewer for technical accuracy and one for writing style. You might also need someone to review a document to see that it reflects company policy. Or when your document is simple, you may simply ask a co-worker to read it over for you and suggest improvements.

A few days in advance of the day scheduled for sending the document out for review, notify your reviewers, reminding them that they are scheduled to review the draft and telling them the date it will arrive and the date they should return it.

## PREPARING THE DRAFT

Your draft of the document need not be perfect, but it should be as complete and as error-free as is reasonably possible. First, you need to prepare a master copy.

Include copies of the illustrations, whether they are final or only rough sketches. Place the photocopy in the text immediately after the page that contains the reference to it, or place all photocopied illustrations for each section at the end of that section.

Mark any errors in text or illustrations on the master copy. When sections are missing, mark the place where they belong and write a note describing their contents and the reason they're not included in the review. For example, your note might read:

> Chapter 5, "How to Change Colors on Your Screen." Not written yet due to lack of a final decision from programming about the user interface design. Will be included in next review.
>
> Art for Figure 9.1, "Drawing of Left-Side Gizmo" with callouts is not ready yet. Will be included in next review.

By marking and describing the missing pieces, you won't waste your reviewers' time. Otherwise, they might search for the material or write unnecessary comments about it. These notes also give the reviewers something to react to—one reviewer may make a suggestion about including a new element in a figure; another may be influential in getting what you need to complete the document.

After you've finished marking the master copy, make copies for all reviewers, a copy for yourself, and one or two more copies for that extra person who inevitably shows up asking for one or for that reviewer who misplaced his or her copy.

You need a copy for yourself for two reasons: You need to know exactly what state the document was in at the time of the review, and you need a clean copy for the corrections you will make when the review is complete.

## WRITING A COVER SHEET

Attach a cover sheet to each review copy, telling reviewers exactly what you want and when. A cover sheet for a review should include:

○ The date you handed out the review copies. (You may need "proof" of the date you started the review.)

○ A list of the reviewers. Reviewers may want to confer with each other, and they can also tell you if you've left anyone off the list.

○ A description of the document or the sections of the document being reviewed.

○ Precise instructions. If you want the reviewers to pay special attention to certain sections, let them know. If, at an early stage, you want them to review content only and ignore writing style, tell them that too. (You may need to add specific notes for individual reviewers.) Tell them how and where to indicate corrections and make comments.

○ The date they must return the review copy and where to send it.

Here's a sample cover sheet for the first review of an instructional manual:

*Cover Sheet*

| | |
|---|---|
| Date: | July 13, 1989 |
| To: | Constance Sukai |
| | John Baxter |
| | Linda Ramirez |
| | Elizabeth Porter |
| From: | Phyllis Rivers |

Contents for First Review: Operator's Manual, Part I, "Setting up the Machine," and Part II, "Basic Operation."

Please note that the positions of figures are marked with a boxed "X" labeled with the figure number. Copies of the figures for each section are included at the end of the section.

You will receive Part III, "Troubleshooting," and Part IV, "Specialized Functions," for review on September 1.

Instructions:

Please read all text and check figures for the enclosed material. I would like you to pay special attention to Chapter 4, "Formatting," as this describes the most complicated and newest operations. Please mark corrections or write comments in red on the appropriate pages and tag each marked page with a paper clip at the top.

Deadline: Return this copy to Phyllis Rivers by 5:00 p.m. on July 26.

## HANDLING REVIEW COMMENTS

Writers have been known to go into shock the first time they look over a stack of marked-up review copies. Even after many reviews, it can be very disheartening to see so many marks made by so many people on so many copies. Remind yourself that many of the comments cover the same point, many may be irrelevant, and some may even be complimentary. Also, remember that, because the goal of a review is to make the document better, you must thoughtfully consider all comments.

## HANDLING MULTIPLE REVIEW COPIES

If you have to go through several review copies, do it methodically to save time and effort. Here are some guidelines:

- Mark all corrections on your master copy.

- Don't make any changes in the document until you've gone through all review copies.

- Read the comments from the most important reviewers first. Usually, these will be your technical experts and your supervisor or project leader.

- Check off each correction or comment in the review copies as you go through them.

- Keep in mind that changes in one section may affect other sections. Mark the other sections immediately or make a note to yourself to do so.

- Initial and date each review copy. You'll then be able to tell each reviewer exactly when you read the comments in the review copy.

## EVALUATING REVIEWERS' COMMENTS

Straightforward corrections of errors are easy to handle. However, three types of review comments deserve special consideration: misunderstandings, editorial comments, and disagreements.

MISUNDERSTANDINGS.   A misunderstanding occurs when a reviewer corrects something that isn't wrong or makes a comment that doesn't seem to make any sense. It's easy to just shrug and ignore these comments; however, they point out problems in your text. If one reader didn't understand what you were saying, others may not either. Read the text over and see whether you can make your meaning clearer.

If the text still seems clear to you after looking it over again, take time to discuss the comment or correction with the reviewer. You may gain a new perspective on the problem.


EDITORIAL COMMENTS.    Editorial comments can be vague, sarcastic, or sometimes even offensive. For the good of the document, writers have to rise above resentment and look for the reason behind the comment.

Some reviewers may write down thoughts as they occur. Most of us carry on an interior monologue when we read something critically, maybe thinking, "Hmmmm, this sentence makes no sense at all," only to discover that the next sentence corrects the problem. But some reviewers, instead of only thinking these thoughts, write them down.

As with misunderstandings, you should talk to the reviewer and try to find out the reasons for any offensive or vague comments you don't understand. Remember that all comments are useful opportunities to improve your document.


DISAGREEMENTS.    With several reviewers, you may run into a disagreement about how a topic is handled or whether it should be handled at all. As the writer, it's up to you to settle these disagreements and decide on the content of your document.

Rank will often make the difference when reviewers disagree. In these cases, you rewrite to suit the person holding most authority as far as your document is concerned.

When all of the reviewers who are in disagreement have equal authority, you have to negotiate. Talk to each person individually. Be positive when you introduce the subject. For instance, you might say something like this: "Your ideas about rewriting this section were helpful, but Cindy also had some good, but very different ideas. Can you help me decide what we should do with this material?" You might also state your preference and then ask for the reviewer's reaction: "I thought I would rewrite this to say. . . Would that be okay with you?"

Occasionally, no one will budge. If each side is adamant, get them together for a discussion. You may discover some underlying reason for the problem, and together you may be able to work out a compromise.

No matter how a dispute is resolved, make a note about how and why you reached a decision on it. You will then be able to refer to your records if the matter is brought up again.

## MAKING CORRECTIONS

After you've finished marking all corrections on your master copy and settled any disagreements, you're ready to make corrections and revisions. Here are some guidelines:

○ Work from your marked-up master copy.

○ Check off the corrections on the master copy as you retype them. If someone else types for you, check the new version against the marked-up master copy.

○ Ask yourself, as you make each correction, whether the correction needs to be made in other places or whether it affects other parts of your document.

○ Check the text around each correction to see that transitions are correct and in place.

# The Final Draft

—Do you know how to revise your drafts step by step?

—Do you know the standard proofreader's marks and how to use them to mark up your draft?

—Do you know how to prepare a final draft for reproduction or printing?

Every writer has to make revisions. You may be lucky enough to have clerical help, editors, and proofreaders who can help you revise your document and make sure it's free of errors. Or you may be on your own, with all of the responsibility. You may be working on a simple document, which will be typed and photocopied for distribution, or a complex document, which will be typeset and printed. (The section, "The Writing Process," in Chapter 2, "Laying the Groundwork," lists all the major steps in creating a document.)

Whatever your responsibilities and whatever the type of document, you'll find that using a methodical approach makes the process of revising less painful.

This chapter contains step-by-step instructions for revising your document, including how to mark it up, how to revise the first and subsequent drafts, and how to prepare the final draft for reproduction or printing.

## MARKING UP A DRAFT

Whether you revise your drafts yourself, give them to a typist or word processor, or deliver them to a typesetter or printer, always use standard proofreader's marks. Figure 15.1 outlines proofreader's marks and Figure 15.2 is a page of marked-up text showing how to use the marks.

Write the changes, using a colored pencil, beside the flawed line, in the margin closest to the error. When you have two or more corrections in a line, list them from left to right and separate them by slant lines (slashes). Print substitutions in the margin and then put a caret (^) in the line to mark the place where the substitution should go. To delete a character, a word, or words, put a delete mark in the margin and a line through the text that should be deleted.

| PROOFREADERS MARKS | IN MARGIN | IN TEXT |
|---|---|---|
| Insert period | ⊙ | M⌄D. |
| comma | ⌃ | Wichita⌄KS |
| colon | ⌃ | To⌄ |
| semicolon | ⌃ | late⌄therefore |
| apostrophe | ⌄ | don⌄t appear |
| quotation marks | ⌄/⌄ | Yes⌄ she said |
| hyphen | /=/ | red⌄marker area |
| parentheses | (/) | listed. See tables.⌄ |
| dash | 1/m | decayed⌄lead is |
| ellipsis | #⊙#⊙#⊙# | going⌄factory |
| space | # | Chapter⌄2 |
| Paragraph | ¶ | lessons.¶Managers will |
| No paragraph | No ¶ | ⌐ The next |
| Run in on same line | (Run in) | After you finish ⌐ cutting the panels |
| Insert here | on/for | Be⌄the alert⌄leakage |
| Make superscript | ⌄² | (x ⌄2) |
| Make subscript | ⌃2 | (x 2⌃) |
| Transpose | (tr) | the⌐of⌐list⌐day |
| Close up | ‿ | Ph.‿D. |
| Spell out | (sp) | sell ②or more |
| Delete | e/e | It⌐is ~~entirely~~ possible |
| Use lower case | (l.c.) | the last W̶atch |
|  |  | the A̶TLANTIC ocean |
| Use capital letter | (cap) | d̲e̲troit, Michigan |
| Use small capitals | (s.c.) | 9:00 a̲.m̲. |
| Set in roman | (Rom) | the cutter (Aurora) |
| Set in italics | (ital) | the word fire̲ |
| Set in boldface | (b.f.) | Note: levers |
| Let it stand (ignore marks) | (stet) | bright ~~and true~~ |

**Figure 15.1.** Proofreader's Marks.

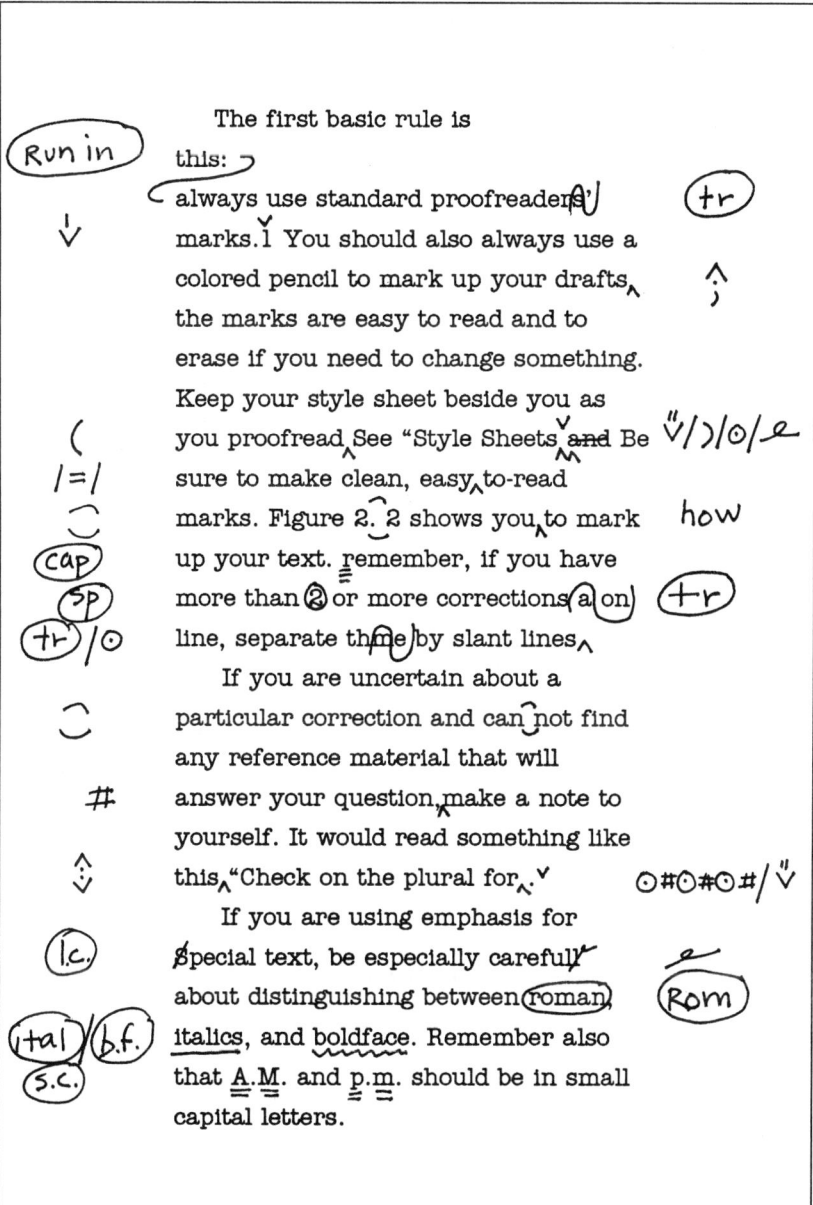

**Figure 15.2.** Example of How to Mark Up Text.

## REVISING THE FIRST DRAFT

1. Use your headings to make an outline. Check to see that you've covered major topics and then check to see that the subtopics are in place.

2. Using the outline, check to see that your topics and subtopics follow a logical order.

3. Read the draft through, checking for clarity, flow, and logical order. Did you introduce each new topic with a topic statement? Did you put in transitions to lead the readers from topic to topic? Did you arrange your ideas in an order that a reader can easily follow?

4. Read the draft again, but this time be ready to take out every unnecessary word. Get rid of the unnecessary prepositional phrases, the redundancies, the ponderous and pompous words. Be merciless.

5. If your word processing software has a style checker, use it.

6. Now, go through the draft again with your style guide in front of you. Is spelling correct and consistent? Have you used that one term you decided on instead of the two or three that could confuse the reader? Are you following the punctuation, capitalization, and the numbers usage defined in the style guide?

## REVISING SECOND AND SUBSEQUENT DRAFTS

1.  If you've had a review, use the master copy (see Chapter 14, "Conducting a Review") to incorporate the corrections into your document.

2.  Be sure all corrections have been made, that they're in the right location, and that no text before or after has been lost.

3.  If you've made major revisions, revise your outline and check to see that topics and subtopics are in place.

4.  If you've changed headings or titles for chapters or sections, make sure you have changed any references to them in other parts of the document.

5.  Read through the revised portions of the document, checking it against your style guide for inconsistencies.

6.  If you are using word processing software that includes a spell checker, use it to correct any misspellings.

7.  Check any completed illustrations, including the text of callouts and titles, to make sure they are correct.

## PREPARING THE FINAL DRAFT

1. Repeat the steps in "Revising Second and Subsequent Drafts."

2. When the illustrations are in place, make sure they are positioned correctly.

3. Be sure the page numbers are in order. (It's surprising how often pages are omitted or duplicated.)

4. Make sure the table of contents lists the correct page numbers.

5. Check all cross-references.

6. Check the headings in the table of contents against the headings in your document.

7. If you have a list of figures or tables, make sure that it lists the correct page numbers.

8. Check the titles in your list of figures and tables against the titles in the text.

9. If you have an index, do a spot check to make sure the page numbers are correct. Check the first five entries and then every fifth one.

10. If you are using word processing software that has a spell checker, use it.

Now you have a clear, engaging, and effective technical document that you can distribute with pride.

# CHAPTER 16

# Sample Documents

SAMPLE MEMO

SAMPLE FEASIBILITY STUDY

We have included two typical documents in their entirety, a simple memo and a longer feasibility study. They include all of the modules that make up a memo and a feasibility study, including the front matter, main text, and back matter.

Keep in mind, however, that documents can vary greatly. Many of your documents will be simpler than the feasibility study included here; others will be more complex. Depending on the document and its goals, some will have fewer, or shorter, modules, and others will have more modules or ones of greater length.

## SAMPLE MEMO

The memo is a typical one. An employee was sent to a conference to gather information. The memo summarizes one of the presentations in which his company was extremely interested.

The writer had no difficulty creating a readers profile; he knows his readers and their level of expertise in the subject. He has given them the technical detail they need to understand what he recommends. He uses semiformal English and a friendly but businesslike tone.

Because the memo is actually a short research report, he has organized it as such. He presented necessary background information before going into the discussion (the order of utility), and gave the readers the big picture before discussing the details (general-to-specific order).

The memo, like a longer report, contains headings and an illustration.

# CCC CONSTRUCTION INC.

## INTEROFFICE MEMO

**To:**        All Group Managers
**From:**      Mitchell Foster
**Date:**      September 9, 1989
**Reference:** Memo dated June 2, 1989 from R. K.
               Levenstein, director of Design and
               Standards, to all group managers,
               regarding frost heave problem
**Subject:**   Suggested Design Standards Change

As you are all aware, we've encountered a frost heave problem in several of our Alaskan projects. At the request of R. K. Levenstein, director of Design and Standards, Diana James and I attended the Cold Regions Engineering Conference held January 24th in Juneau, Alaska. Diana and I attended this conference, held annually for contractors doing business in Alaska, specifically to hear one presentation, "Preventing Frost Heave in Concrete Slabs." This presentation was delivered by Joel Geffs of Arctic Construction, one of the most experienced and competent general contractors building in cold regions. For your information, here is a summary of Mr. Geffs' presentation. (The presentation is attached if you want to read it in its entirety.)

PREVENTING FROST HEAVE IN CONCRETE SLABS

*Frost heave* is a term for damage to concrete slabs caused by the cycle of freezing and thawing that happens in arctic regions. The combination of changing temperatures and the high water table found in tundra areas frequently results in the accumulation of surface water in warmer temperatures

2

and in ice lenses in colder temperatures. These changing soil conditions tend to support concrete slabs unevenly, causing the slab to rise, sag, and crack.

GENERAL DESIGN

To prevent the frost heave problem, Arctic Construction uses the design illustrated on the following page.

This design features a standard reinforced 4- to 6-inch concrete slab. The building walls are not supported by the slab, but rather by the concrete footing below. This is the same general design that we use for our buildings. However, note that in the illustration the slab is positioned on a raised soil base 6 to 8 inches thick. We also use a base of this thickness, but have never raised the base above ground level.

Base Materials

Arctic recommends that the base consist of coarse soils with large pore sizes, containing no more than 5 percent (by weight) of particles less than two millimeters in diameter. In other words, no more than five percent of the base soil should be able to pass through a No. 200 mesh sieve. In addition to controlling the particle size of the base soil, Arctic regularly improves the drainage by compacting the base to at least 90 percent of Modified Procter Density. Although in the past we have made a general attempt to use sand or gravel as a base, and we've also compacted the base somewhat, our standards for particle size and compaction have never been specified.

Vapor Barrier

Most construction companies, including ours, use a polyethylene sheet as a vapor barrier beneath concrete slabs. Mr. Geffs stated that in Arctic's experience, this type of sheet

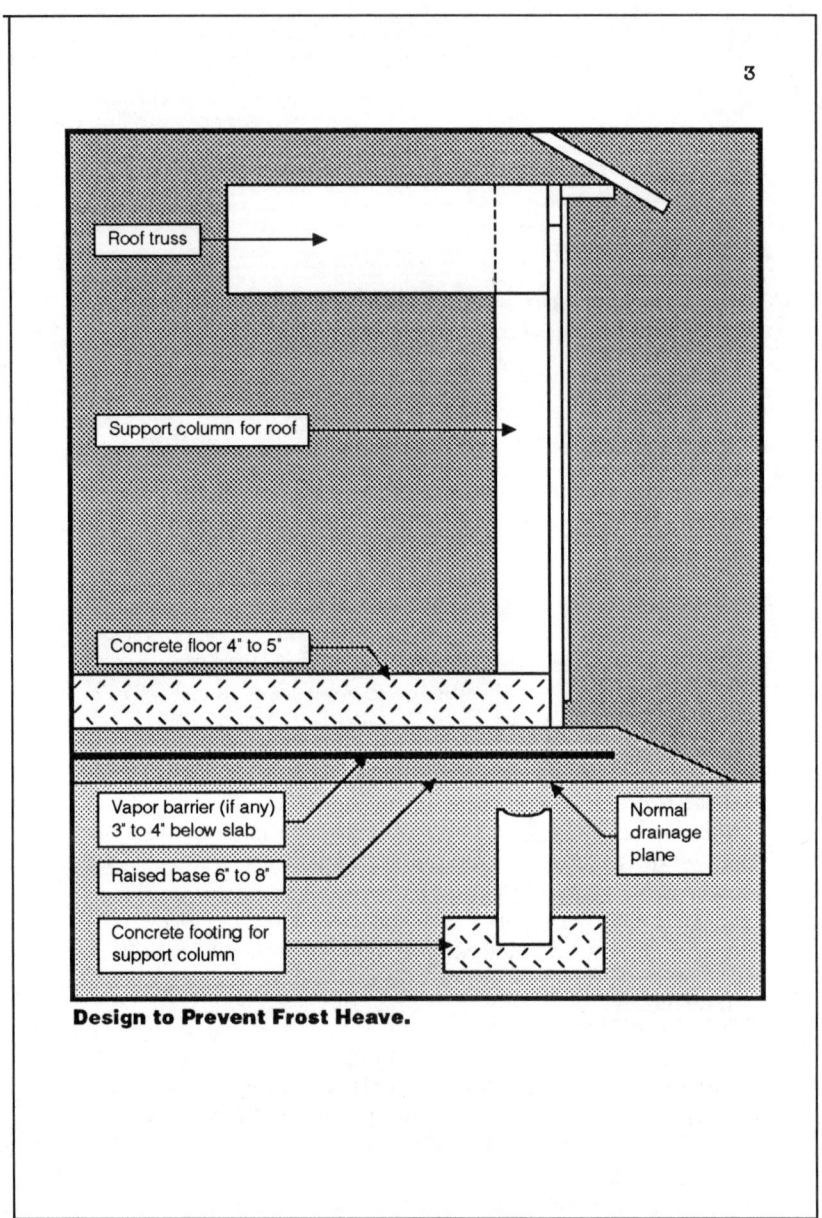

3

**Design to Prevent Frost Heave.**

4

could be beneficial only if placed three to four inches below the slab and sandwiched between a layer of sand above and coarse fill below. Placing a plastic sheet directly below the concrete, he said, can cause uneven drying of the concrete, resulting in buckling of the slab.

RECOMMENDATIONS

I recommend that we adopt Arctic's standard design for all concrete slab floors installed in Alaska or Northern Canada. I also recommend that we revise our blueprints for the upcoming Iceberg Valley project to incorporate a raised base and a lowered plastic sheet for all concrete slabs. We'll discuss adopting these standards and revising blueprints at the next management meeting.

| MF: | pg |
| --- | --- |
| cc: | Farley Wright |
| | Theresa Hanley |
| | M. K. Martin |
| | Winifred Bauer |
| | T. Colocos |
| Attachment: | "Preventing Frost Heave in Concrete Slabs" |

## SAMPLE FEASIBILITY STUDY

The feasibility study describes the pros and cons of buying and installing a new computer system for a company that is having problems with its present system.

This writer also knows her readers; they are her fellow managers. Some of them have extensive knowledge of the subject matter, some do not. She has written the report to fill all of their needs, providing background, definitions, and adequate descriptions. She uses semiformal English and a friendly but businesslike tone.

This feasibility study follows the standard pattern of typical feasibility studies. In addition, the writer uses one of the common logical orders to organize her topics. In the description of the existing system, she discusses its problems, beginning with the most important ones (the order of descending importance). Later the writer uses this same order to arrange the discussion of the new system's potential benefits.

The feasibility study contains illustrations and a table of data in an appendix.

We've added some headings in the introduction so that the modules will be apparent, but because some of the modules are extremely short, the introduction would have worked just as well without headings.

THE FEASIBILITY OF PURCHASING

A NEW COMPUTER SYSTEM

February 15, 1989

Submitted by: Alma Foster
Manager, Operations

# Norwest Corporation

February 15, 1989

Dear Manager:

The Computer Study Committee has completed its initial research into the feasibility of purchasing a new computer system before the end of the quarter. The enclosed report discusses their findings.

Only one supplier, Hard&Soft Solutions, proposed a system that fell within our price range. The configuration is typical of what is available today and offers all of the basic features we are seeking. This report analyzes the feasibility of replacing our old, outdated system with a system similar to the one that Hard&Soft recommends.

The subject of our computer system is on the agenda for the managers meeting in March, and we will discuss our options at that time.

Sincerely,


Ruth Hoolahan
Manager, Communications

cc:   Mike Spangler
      Steve Guild
      Rebecca Chu
      Ren Pope
      Susan Martinez
      Ike McCarley

ii

## CONTENTS

iii

iv

## LIST OF FIGURES

v

## TERMS

**BIOS**

Basic Input/Output System. The part of the computer that controls reading and writing to disks, printers, and any other input/output devices.

**High-density disks**

Sometimes called double-density disks or diskettes. Disks that can hold more bytes of information than low-density disks. Many high-density disks are also double-sided disks. High-density disks can be read only by high-density drives.

**Low-density disks**

Disks (or diskettes) that hold fewer bytes of information than high-density disks. Low-density disks can be read by either high-density or low-density drives.

**Resolution**

Resolution refers to the number of pixels (picture elements or "dots") on a monitor screen or on a printed page. The higher the number of pixels, the higher the resolution, and the better the quality of output.

**Zero-wait state**

A feature of new computers in which the computer processes commands immediately, rather than waiting for a specified period of time.

vi

## ABSTRACT

We are considering the feasibility of replacing our outdated system of personal computers with a new system. The Computer Study Committee found only one vendor, Hard&Soft Solutions, who could supply a system that met our requirements at our price.

The proposed system would replace our present computers and printers with new ones capable of high-speed processing, graphics capabilities, high-resolution printing, and internal compatibility. This would result in improved efficiency, savings, and better relations with our customers and other business associates.

The final cost is as follows:

| | |
|---|---|
| New system | $72,950.00 |
| New software | 2,000.00 |
| Charitable deduction | (39,000.00) |
| Cost | $35,950.00 |

We should replace our present system now, either purchasing the proposed system or trying to negotiate better prices from two additional vendors to give us more options.

1

## INTRODUCTION

### Topic and Goal of this Report

The goal of this report is to determine whether it's feasible to purchase a new computer system at this time to replace our present, badly outdated computer system.

### Intended Readers

The Computer Study Committee wrote this report to assist the company managers who will decide whether or not to replace the old computer system.

### Sources of Information

Information used in this report was provided by our company managers and by Suzanne Beauchamp of Hard&Soft Solutions.

### Background

We have known for some time that our current system of personal computers is out of date and that it hampers our ability to communicate with and compete with other companies. To find the best solution for our computer problems, G. G. Hopkins, director of operations, formed a Computer Study Committee, consisting of Ren Pope, Ruth Hoolahan, and Mike Spangler.

The committee, working with the board of directors, determined the maximum price the company could spend for a new computer system. The committee requested information from ten local computer vendors. Based on this information, the committee then asked three local computer vendors to submit proposals. The only proposal that was in our price range came from Hard&Soft Solutions, a well-known vendor with a good reputation in our area. This report discusses the feasibility of implementing Hard&Soft's proposed configuration.

**DISCUSSION**

**Need Assessment**

<u>Description of Existing System.</u> We have 26 personal computers and 7 printers in use throughout the company:

| | |
|---|---|
| Accounting | 5 EZ-X computers |
| | 2 MT1200 printers |
| Marketing | 3 MicroZip computers |
| | 1 MT1200 printer |
| All Other Groups | 4 EZ-X computers |
| | 14 MicroZip computers |
| | 4 FluidT printers |

Our managers and clerical staff use these computers and printers for all our correspondence and bookkeeping tasks. Figure 1 shows the location of our computers and printers.

Our computers can read only low-density disks, the only disks available at the time we purchased our system. In addition, our computers don't have graphics cards, which are now widely used in computers throughout the industry.

<u>Description of Problems.</u> Generally speaking, our existing computer system has served us quite well over the past eight years. However, our system has fallen behind developments in the computer industry, in which high-density disks and graphics cards have become standard equipment. Due to this disparity, we have increasingly encountered the following problems in the last two years:

- Our computers can't read high-density disks. High-density disks are rapidly becoming the industry standard because many of the new and powerful software programs don't fit on a low-density disk.
- Our computers can't produce high-quality graphics because our system doesn't have graphics cards or high-resolution screens.

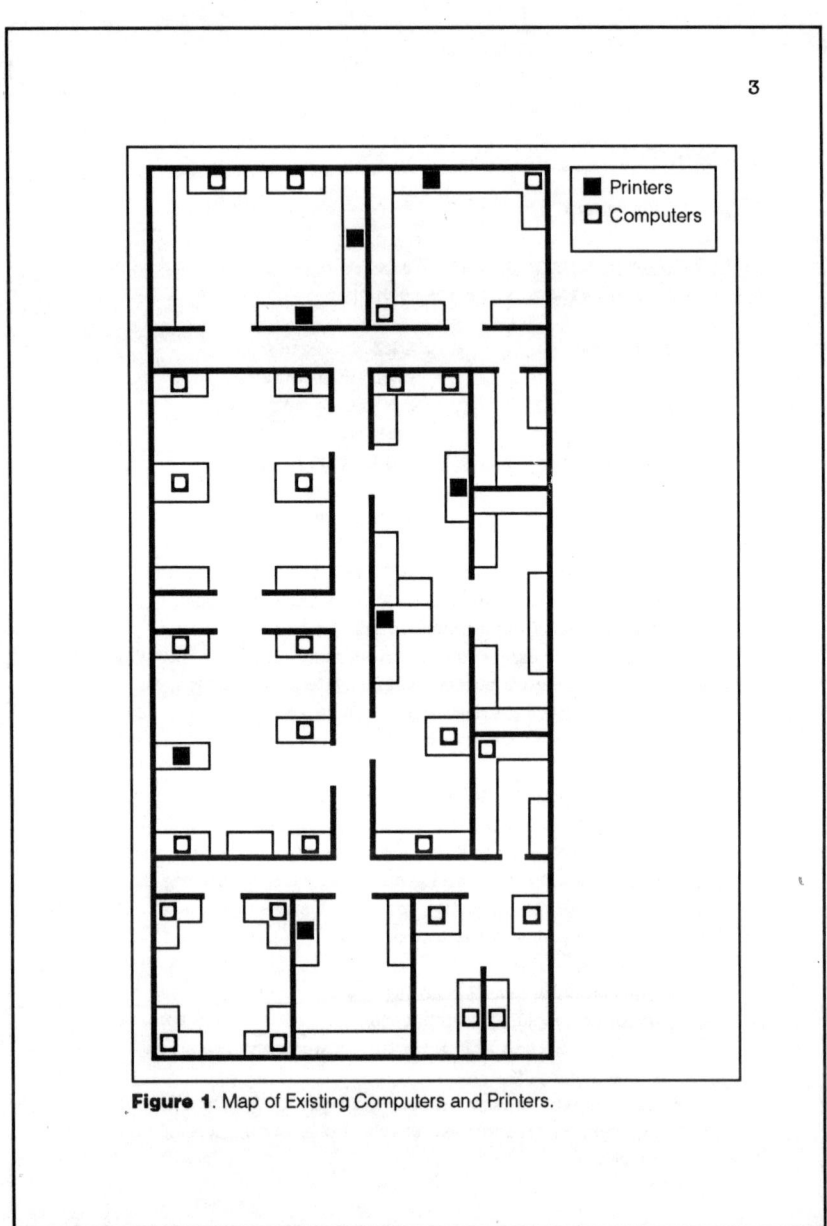

**Figure 1**. Map of Existing Computers and Printers.

4

- Our printers can't print high-quality graphics because they do not print at high resolution.
- Our EZ-X computers aren't compatible with our MicroZip computers.
- Our limited number of printers can no longer handle the increasing volume of our printing needs.

These problems affect the productivity levels and capacity for growth in our company. Because our computers can't read high-density disks, many divisions of the company work with older versions of software instead of new, more powerful versions.

We have been forced to hire outside consultants to produce graphics for our brochures and presentations because our computer system can't produce high-quality graphics.

Because of the compatibility problem, we spend too much time translating disks. One EZ-X computer and one MicroZip computer, linked by cable, are dedicated to moving information from computer to computer.

The limited number of printers (the ratio is nearly four computers to one printer) causes delays in our production of printed material. Every time a printer breaks down, which happens frequently, we have costly overtime. The Appendix summarizes the frequency, duration, and cost of computer breakdowns.

**Description of Proposed Computer System**
Suzanne Beauchamp of Hard&Soft Solutions recommends that we purchase 28 new SuperCeed computer packages, 5 new SpeeDemon printers, and a Z5000 scanner from Hard&Soft Solutions Company.

We'll move the modem cards in our present computers to the new computers, and we'll keep all of our existing printers.

Proposed Placement. Twenty-six of the purchased computers will replace our existing computers. We will place the remaining two computers in our machine room for use by our summer interns, temporary employees, or staff members without other access to computers.

Each work group will keep the printers currently assigned to them. We will place the five new printers strategically within work groups. Figure 2 shows the proposed placement of new equipment.

<u>Computers and Monitors.</u> The SuperCeed computer comes with the GGG graphics card, which computer experts (*Comp-YOU-T Magazine* testing labs and *PC Value Reports*) rate as the best graphics card on the market today.

Each computer is equipped with a 40MB hard disk, one high-density disk drive, one low-density disk drive, and eight empty expansion slots. Each package also includes the latest version of the SuperCeed operating system and the BAZIK programming language, two serial ports, one parallel port, and a mouse. These computers have what is known as a zero-wait state, which means that they can process data very quickly.

The SuperCeed computer also comes with a color monitor, which, because of its high-resolution screen, has outstanding graphics capabilities.

<u>Printers.</u> The SpeeDemon printers are high-resolution laser printers, capable of producing text and graphics of a quality comparable to typeset text and graphics. These printers can print in three different colors and can print on paper or transparencies. The package includes printer cables. The printers come with 12 fonts installed and can use 48 other fonts, which can be purchased on 5.25-inch or 3.5-inch disks from Hard&Soft.

<u>Scanner.</u> The Z5000 scanner can "read" printed text and graphics (such as newspaper articles, book pages, and word-processed reports) and transfer the printed information to a computer file, which we can then edit, manipulate, and print like any other computer file.

6

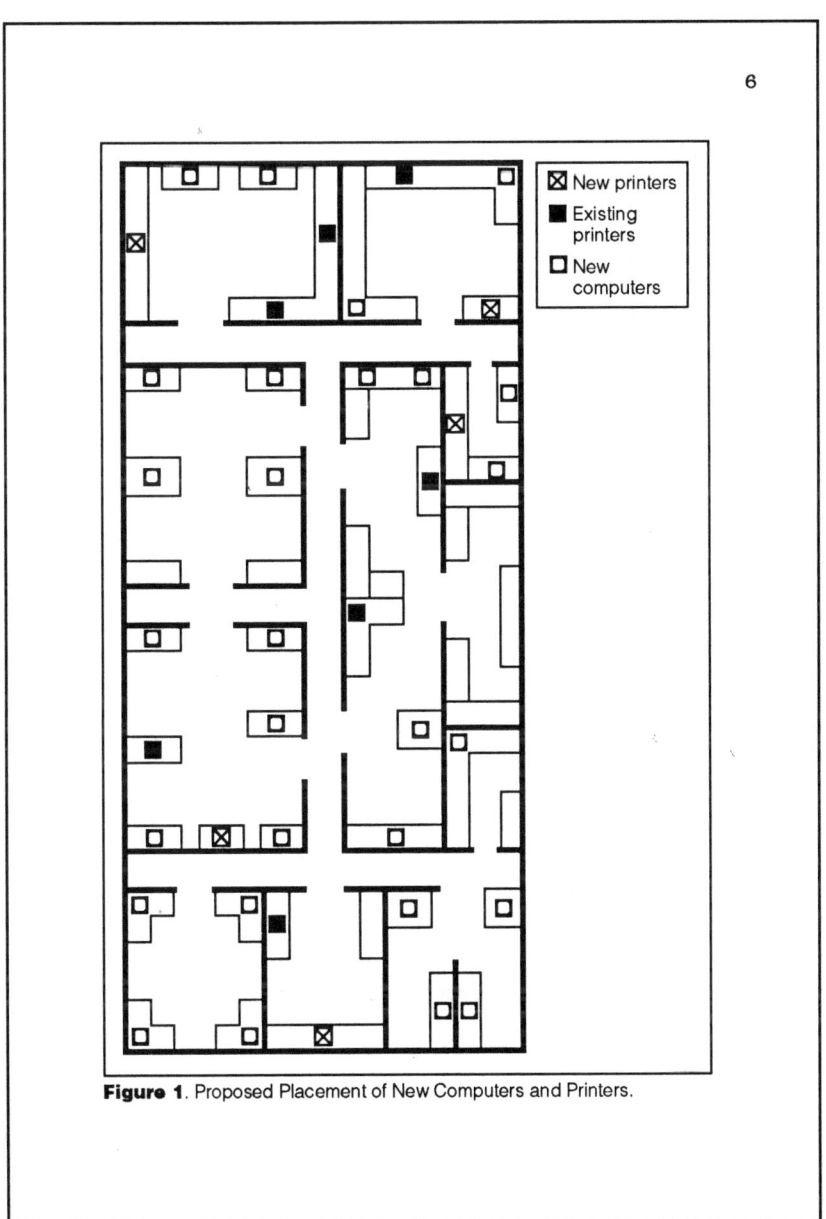

**Figure 1**. Proposed Placement of New Computers and Printers.

Software Bonus. Because of the magnitude of our order, Hard&Soft Solutions is offering us a special bonus: a free copy of the Present! software program, which produces slides by "capturing" the graphics and text produced on the monitor screen.

Service Contract. Hard&Soft's package price includes a one-year service contract. After the first year, the annual cost of the service contract would be $1500. Hard&Soft Solutions has an extensive service department and promises that it will either take care of problems within 24 hours, or, if repairs should take longer, loan us replacement equipment.

**Potential Benefits**

The benefits of purchasing the new computers and printers can be summed up by saying that we can accommodate our current needs while providing room for future growth. We'll improve the quality of our graphics, increase productivity, and realize savings as outlined in the following sections.

Improved Quality. New graphics capabilities will allow us to produce quality graphics (including slides) for presentations, brochures, annual reports, and advertising fliers. Compare Figure 3, which shows a chart produced using our best computers and printers, with Figure 4, a chart produced using the proposed system.

Increased Productivity. The new computers are up to four times faster than our current computers. Also, because they allow printing in the background, you can continue to use them while they send files to the printer. This will dramatically increase productivity, especially among the clerical and word-processing staff, who currently cannot use their computers for other tasks when they're printing a document.

The new computers are equipped with both high-density and low-density drives that will also increase our productivity. We'll be able to upgrade to the new versions of our current software programs

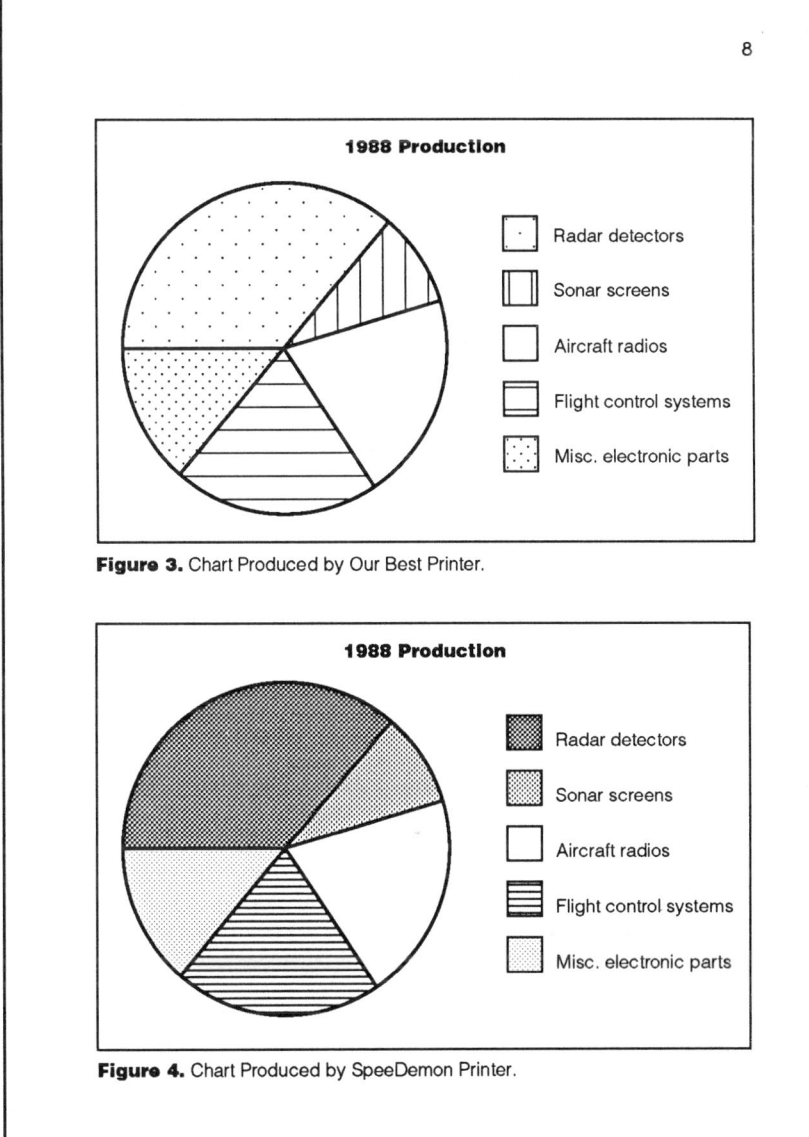

8

**1988 Production**

- Radar detectors
- Sonar screens
- Aircraft radios
- Flight control systems
- Misc. electronic parts

**Figure 3.** Chart Produced by Our Best Printer.

**1988 Production**

- Radar detectors
- Sonar screens
- Aircraft radios
- Flight control systems
- Misc. electronic parts

**Figure 4.** Chart Produced by SpeeDemon Printer.

(which run only on high-density drives) and still be able to access the existing information currently stored on our low-density disks. The new high-density drives will also give us more flexibility in sending and receiving disks to and from our outside vendors and project partners, who have often expressed annoyance because we still require low-density disks.

The addition of five printers also means an increase in productivity. We can print documents as soon as they are completed, rather than queueing them for the printer. We'll continue to use our existing printers to print draft copies, and then produce final copies on the new printers.

The recommended computer configuration comes with a free one-year service contract. Since Hard&Soft Solutions promises to either take care of problems within 24 hours, or, if repairs will take longer, loan us replacement equipment, we should have fewer breakdowns with a shorter duration, which will also improve productivity.

<u>Savings.</u> We can realize savings with the new system in several areas.

We will no longer have to use typesetting services; the new printers produce high-quality text.

Hiring outside vendors to produce our graphics, duplicate advertising photos, and paste up master copies will no longer be necessary. We can use page-layout software to produce our own in-house graphics (including slides) for presentations, brochures, annual reports, and advertising fliers. The savings in time and money will be considerable.

Because all the new computers are compatible, we will eliminate the time and expense involved in translating disks.

The addition of the five new printers will also mean savings. Our system will no longer be overloaded. We can expect fewer breakdowns and consequently much less overtime.

### Impact of Purchasing Proposed System

Replacing our present computer system with a new one will impact on both existing programs and future plans.

10

Impact on Existing Programs. The new system would have a beneficial impact on all of our programs as outlined in the section "Potential Benefits" above. It would impact our current operations for a brief period in three areas:

Installation time
Coordination time
Training time

*Installation Time.* The impact on our current operations, because of time needed for installation, is fairly minimal. Hard&Soft Solutions will format the hard disks before delivering the computers and will set up and test the computers and printers for us. Hard&Soft Solutions will also remove modem cards from old computers and install them in the new ones. We conservatively estimate two hours of down time per computer, during which time Hard&Soft Solutions will set up each computer and printer. We'll arrange the setup time to coincide with our normal lunch hour so as to minimize the loss of computer time.

Some time will also be spent on copying software and data from our old computers onto floppy disks, erasing the old hard disks (for security reasons), then copying the software and data from the floppy disks onto the new computers. We estimate this will take one person about two hours per computer: one hour to back up the old computers and erase the hard disks, and one hour to transfer the data onto the new computers.

The installation of the five new printers will take Hard&Soft Solutions some time, but will have little impact on our current operations. We can use our old printers while the new ones are being installed.

*Coordination Time.* The greatest impact on our current operations will be in time spent in coordination. There will inevitably be some time and effort involved in informing our staff, communicating with Hard&Soft, and collecting and shipping our old computers. We estimate 24 hours of one person's time as liaison between the company and outside parties.

*Training Time.* Training time to learn to use the new computers is negligible and will have little impact on our current operations. We can use our current software until it's convenient to upgrade to new versions. Keyboards and basic operations for the new computers are exactly the same as those for our old computers, so our employees do not have to learn new methods.

The SpeeDemon printers, the Z5000 scanner, and the Present! software package are new equipment to us, so our staff will have to learn to operate and service the hardware and learn how to use the software. Hard&Soft Solutions offers monthly seminars on the use of both hardware and software. According to the terms of our service contract, we can send a maximum of 10 employees per month at no additional cost to us.

When we make the decision to purchase a page-layout program, we'll have to budget hours for training at that time.

Impact on Future Plans. The purchase of the proposed system would improve our ability to compete for business and also speed up our proposal process. We expect that it will improve business in the future, although we have no hard and fast data to confirm our expectations.

The new system will definitely have an impact on our expansion plans. If we experience rapid expansion or open branch offices, we would have the option of linking the new computers into a network. We could share files more easily among different offices, and we could create a centralized computer security system to track computer use throughout the company.

12

**Alternatives**

The alternatives to purchasing the Hard&Soft Solutions package are to:

- purchase a package from another supplier.
- upgrade our current system.
- continue operating with our current system.

<u>Purchasing from Another Supplier.</u> We talked to ten local computer suppliers when we did our research for this report. Hard&Soft Solutions offered the best price for a package that meets our needs.

If we want to consider more than one supplier and still stay within our budget, we could try to negotiate a better deal with the other two vendors who submitted proposals over our top price. Or, if expanding our options really seemed necessary, we might consider allocating more money for the purchase.

<u>Upgrading Our Current System.</u> We have investigated the possibility of upgrading our existing computers. Experts tell us that we can't install high-density disk drives because the BIOS (Basic Input/Output System), the heart of the computers, can't interface with new drives. We could install graphics cards and buy new high-resolution monitors for our existing computers, but because all expansion slots in our existing computers are filled, we would have to sacrifice another benefit (such as an extra serial port, extra memory, and in a few cases, modem cards) to make a slot available for the graphics card.

<u>Impact of No Action.</u> If we remain with our current system, we'll continue to be limited in our operations, as discussed in the "Background" section at the beginning of this report. Quite possibly we may eventually lose a portion of our business because we can't coordinate with outside companies who are using newer equipment.

Deferring the purchase for another six months is not an advisable alternative because prices for computer systems will inevitably go up.

### 13

### Risks

The only risk we can foresee in the purchase of the new computer system is the speed at which the computer industry changes. At this time, the proposed system would seem to fulfill our needs for many years to come. However, it is impossible to foresee new developments that could outdate a computer system.

### Costs

The cost of the new system is $72,950.00. This includes all installation costs, as well as a one-year service contract with Hard&Soft Solutions company. Our current insurance coverage is adequate to protect our investment.

To buy new versions of our existing software programs and a new page-layout program, we estimate a maximum of $2,000.00.

We can further offset the cost if we donate our existing computers to the local schools. Our accountants tell us that we can take a charitable tax deduction of $1,500.00 per computer, resulting in a total deduction of $39,000.00.

To sum up:

| | |
|---|---|
| Cost of package | $72,950.00 |
| New software | 2,000.00 |
| Charitable tax deduction | (39,000.00) |
| | |
| Final cost | $35,950.00 |

While this is still a substantial investment for the company, we believe that increased productivity will quickly make up for this cost.

### CONCLUSION

We need a new computer system as soon as possible. Our current system is outdated and limits our operations and competitiveness. Hard&Soft Solutions is offering us a package that meets our current needs while allowing a great deal of room for future growth.

We'll discuss whether or not to proceed with the purchase of a new system at the manager's meeting in March.

14

## APPENDIX

The following table summarizes the cost of overtime due to printer breakdowns in the past year.

| Date of Breakdown | Duration of Breakdown | Cost of Overtime |
|---|---|---|
| January 15 | 6 hours | $250.00 |
| January 22–23 | 8 hours | 510.00 |
| February 13 | 4 hours | 190.00 |
| April 4–6 | 20 hours | 1300.00 |
| July 9 | 2 hours | 80.00 |
| September 23–24 | 10 hours | 720.00 |
| October 16 | 5 hours | 220.00 |
| November 3 | 6 hours | 350.00 |
| Totals | 61 hours | $3620.00 |

15

## REFERENCES

"State-of-the-Art Computers," *COMP-YOU-T Magazine*, Vol. XX, March 1989.

"Best Computer Buys," *PC Value Reports*, Vol. 22, February 1989.

16

## INDEX

18

# Mechanics of Style

For your convenience, we have summarized the rules and conventions for spelling and punctuation, abbreviations, capitalization, and for using numbers and symbols. For a list of books that contain detailed guidelines on style, see "Recommended Reference Books."

## SPELLING AND PUNCTUATION

### PLURALS

The best way to make sure you are spelling a plural correctly is to look it up in the dictionary. But here are examples that illustrate the rules.

*Proper names*

four Janes and three Sallys

inquired of the Joneses

*Exceptions (because of pronunciation)*

thirteen King Louis

twelve chamois

*Italicized words*

four *Herald*s

two *au revoir*s

*Letters*

the three Rs
    but A's, S's and I's

Bs and Cs

B's and C's

*Coinages*

two brass-ring-winners

*Acronyms*

CODs

*Numbers*

the early 1970s

*Abbreviations*

M.A.'s

Ph.D.'s

## POSSESSIVES

Here are examples showing current usage for apostrophes:

*Singular nouns*

cat's tail

supervisor's duties

*Plural nouns*

supervisors' duties

*Nouns with s or other sibilants*

Watts's methods

Marx's theories

Morales' statement (because of pronunciation)

*Linked nouns*

Brown and Black's case

*Pronouns*

its finale (It's a solid start.)

one's position

## HYPHENATED AND COMPOUND WORDS

To hyphenate or not to hyphenate, that is the question. The current wisdom is to unite words that convey a single idea such as:

airborne

filename

handheld

database

In some cases, however, compound words still keep the hyphen. Rules for compound words include:

*Series of words with a common base*

one- and two-sided diskettes

small- and large-sized logs

*Numeral-unit adjectives*

12-inch ruler

20-ring pole

*Aid to meaning or pronunciation*

right-of-way

up-to-standard methods

*Adjectives in front of word they modify*

factory-assembled equipment

red-toned tint

*(except words ending in* ly *and comparatives)*

wholly owned subsidiary

most read edition

*Improvisations*

a right-on-the-mark estimate

## ITALICS AND QUOTATION MARKS

Words that need special emphasis are sometimes enclosed in quotation marks and sometimes italicized.

These examples illustrate several rules for italicizing words. (Because many typewriters and computer printers do not have italic type, it is common practice to underline those words that should appear in italics.)

*Foreign and scientific words*

*faux pas*

*ad nauseum*

*mycobacterium tuberculosis*

*Emphasis and special use*

Do *not* touch the lead wire.

Enter the password *time*.

The general subject of such relationships is called *kinematics*.

*Books, pamphlets, periodicals*

If you want further information, read *Guide to Operations* by Sally Smith.

The source was the *Journal of Mathematics*.

Here are examples that illustrate the rules for quotation marks:

*Articles, lectures, and speeches*

Read "Going Whole Hog" by Joseph Green.

I attended Smith's lecture, "Clean Air for Tomorrow."

*Courses*

The Education Department recommends their course "Beginning BASIC."

*Chapters*

For more information, see "Chapter One: Pros and Cons."

*Attributions*

"We take the high road," Jones said.

She told the audience, "We will win this war."

*Attributions with semicolons*

The specifications say "superior grade or better"; however, they do not indicate who will make this judgment.

*Attributions with colons*

They wanted "freebies": work performed for no charge.

*Attributions with question marks*

"What sets it apart?" asked the supervisors.

Why did the manager want "all contract engineers moved"?

*Attributions with exclamation points*

"Absolutely nothing!" he answered.

He actually accused them of "sabotage"!

# ABBREVIATIONS

## COMMON ABBREVIATIONS

These examples are abbreviation guidelines:

*Dates*

8/31/34 (in a table or other display)

August 31, 1934 (in text)

*For the word* per

ft/s (feet per second)

*States*

Wichita, KS (outside address, envelope)

Wichita, Kansas (inside address or text)

*Titles*

Gen. Buck Rogers; but General Jones (last name only)

*Plurals of courtesy titles*

Messrs. (Mr.)

Mmes. (Miss or Ms.)

Ms. (Ms.)

*Plurals with periods*

The M.D.'s agreed to the plan.

*Contractions*

Intl. *not* Int'l (for *International*)

## SCIENTIFIC AND TECHNICAL ABBREVIATIONS

These are some common abbreviations used in science and technology, including units of measurement:

| | |
|---|---|
| A, angstrom | kg, kilogram |
| AC, alternating current | kw, kilowatt |
| amp, ampere | kwh, kilowatt hour |
| at wt, atomic weight | l, liter |
| az, azimuth | lat, latitude |
| bbl., barrel | lb., pound |
| Btu, British thermal unit | lin, linear |
| C, Celsius | long, longitude |
| CAL, calorie (large) | log, logarithm |
| cal, calorie (small) | m, meter |
| cc, cubic centimeter | max, maximum |
| circ, circumference | mg, milligram |
| cm, centimeter | mi., mile |
| cps, cycles per second | min, minute |
| cu, cubic | MP, melting point |
| DC, direct current | MPH, miles per hour |
| FM, frequency modulation | N or n, number |
| ft., foot | neg, negative |
| gal., gallon | oz., ounce |
| gr., grain | pt., pint |
| HP, horsepower | rd., rod |
| in., inch | yd., yard |

## CAPITALIZATION

Paying attention to the rules of capitalization is another way to add consistency and gain your readers' confidence. Here are some examples for the rules of capitalization.

| | |
|---|---|
| *Proper nouns* | Cynthia Kane |
| *Names of languages* | Spanish |
| *Days of the week* | Tuesday |
| *The months* | February |
| *Historical events* | World War II |
| *Names of buildings* | Chrysler Building |
| *Titles before a name* | Bishop Brown |
| *Titles after a name* | J. Smith, president of the college |
| *Titles of books* | *Words into Type* |
| *Titles of chapters* | Chapter 4 |
| *Holidays* | Memorial Day |
| *Organizations* | Veterans of Foreign Wars |
| *General groups* | senior citizens |
| *College classes* | sophomore |
| *Races and nationalities* | Polish |
| *Important documents* | Magna Carta |
| *Specific locations* | the Northwest |
| *Directions* | north, west, southeast |
| *Seasons* | winter, spring |
| *Adjectives from proper nouns* | Wagnerian opera |

In titles of books and films as well as headings in documents, capitalize the first word and all other words except articles and prepositions. For example:

> The Land and Literature of England
>
> The Role of the Manager

## NUMBERS AND SYMBOLS

Here are examples that illustrate the rules for spelling out numbers (ten) and using numerals (10):

*First word in sentence*

Ten percent of the crew failed the test.

*Less than 10*

Choose at least five test cases.

*Less than 10 but with larger numbers*

Send them 5 black and 22 red versions.

*More than 10*

They need 18 sites.

*A round and indefinite number*

Did you say between one and two hundred panels?

*Before units of time, measurement, or money*

55 years

5 o'clock or 5:00

5 × 6 feet

200 volts

1:4

$15.00

*Fraction standing alone or followed by* of a *or* of an

one-eighth inch

two-thirds of a log

*Before a modifier that contains a figure*

five 14-inch boards

*A part of a book*

Chapter 2, page 33

Table III

*Five digits or more*

1000

10,155

360,270

*Million and billion*

560 million

12 billion

*Equations*

$6 \times 10 = 60$

*Numbers*

$6 \times 10^2$

These examples show the correct usage for symbols:

| | |
|---|---|
| *X (magnification)* | 30X |
| *x (multiplication)* | $2 \times 4 = 8$ |
| *x (number)* | $2x20^3$ |
| *Percentage (text)* | The percentage given was 14 percent |
| *Percentage (data)* | 90% |
| *Abbreviations* | 512K, 2D and 3D |
| *Degree (in directions)* | 45°21′10″E |
| *Degree (temperature)* | 32°F |
| *Degree (angle)* | 45 deg or 45-degree angle |
| *Measurements* | 12 ft 6 in (not 12′6″) |

# Recommended
# Reference Books

## ABRIDGED AND STANDARD DICTIONARIES

*Funk and Wagnall's Standard College Dictionary.* New York: Harper & Row Publishers, Inc., 1984. One of the better abridged dictionaries.

Shaw, Harry. *Dictionary of Problem Words and Expressions,* Revised Edition. New York: McGraw-Hill Book Company, 1987. A handy guide to the proper usage of more than 1,500 tricky words and phrases.

*The Random House College Dictionary.* Revised Edition. New York: Random House, Inc., 1987. A lot of entries for a desk dictionary.

*Webster's Ninth New Collegiate Dictionary,* 9th ed. Merriam-Webster Inc., 1985. A standard abridged dictionary.

*Webster's Third New International Dictionary,* Unabridged: The Great Library of the English Language. Merriam-Webster Inc., 1986. A standard unabridged dictionary.

## STYLE GUIDES

*The Chicago Manual of Style.* 13th ed. Chicago and London: The University of Chicago Press, 1982. A standard reference for questions on style. Perhaps *the* most widely used style guide.

Skillin, M. and Gay, R. *Words into Type.* 3rd ed. Englewood Cliffs, N.J.: Prentice-Hall, Inc., 1974. Another style guide in wide use.

Jordan, Lewis. *The New York Times Manual of Style and Usage.* New York: Times Books, 1982. A complete and easy-to-use style guide.

## BOOKS ON COMPOSITION, USAGE, AND WRITING

Bates, Jefferson D. *Writing with Precision.* Washington, D.C.: Acropolis Books, Ltd. 1985. A clear and thorough guide to writing.

Cook, Claire Kehrwald. *Line by Line: The MLA's Guide to Improving Your Writing.* Boston: Houghton Mifflin Company, 1985. In-depth guide to improving your writing.

Ebbett, Wilma R. and Ebbett, David R. *Writer's Guide and Index to English.* 7th ed. Chicago: Scott, Foresman and Company, 1982. A comprehensive and helpful guide for writers.

Montgomery, Michael and Stratton, John. *The Writer's Hotline Handbook: A Guide to Good Usage and Effective Writing.* New York and Scarborough, Ontario: New American Library, 1981. An easy-to-use guide to usage and writing.

Strunk, William, Jr. and White, E. B. *The Elements of Style.* 3rd ed. New York: The Macmillan Company, 1979. A brief guide to writing plain English.

# INDEX